The StarChild Channels

The Crystal Skull from Beyond the Stars

Linda Hostalek, D.O.

Copyright, 2013

Hostalek press
Linda Hostalek D.O.

Photos taken by Linda Hostalek D.O., copyright 2013

The King/Laialani photo courtesy of the Crystal Skull Explorers, Joshua Shapiro and Katrina Head

Prologue

Crystal skulls have held a great fascination for centuries. Through the legends of other worlds and mysticism, the field has grown over the past few years in accordance with 5the culmination of the Mayan calendar's ending date. Many have misunderstood this calendar to be the end of the world as we know it. It is rather, a new beginning, one in which the crystal skulls have a part to play. A reset of sorts, they contain unique consciousness' as anyone who has ever been honored to be a guardian of one will attest. It is now time to begin to speak to those beings who's consciousness has been revealed through the various skulls now making themselves known.

On a physical level, there are new, old and ancient skulls. The new ones are shaped by skilled carvers with great care. Some are hand carved, while others are now made via an exact machining process. Made out of a variety of materials, they have become very popular over the recent past, with peaked interest of the connection between the end of the Mayan calendar and the crystal skulls. Movies, such as the Indiana Jones (r) series, have also increased interest in these mystical entities.

Being made of natural stone, the beings will resonate with the elemental forces they are created from. This allows the property of energy transmission to occur, and is one way in which crystal skulls are programmed with information. The crystalline structure creates a piezo-electric effect that carries information through the energetic forces, such as telluric currents that are similar to the meridians of the earth. In addition, the intention that goes into each piece as it is carved greatly affects the energy of the finished skull. The skull is already in there, the carvers just liberate it the same way a great artist reveals the sculpture within the block of marble. The time is now for these beings' desire to be revealed to the world. They carry great information for the evolution of the ascension of the multiverse. These 'new' skulls, contain the ancient knowledge that is present in their very materials. They can also be 'programmed,' much in the same way that quartz crystals can be. One can find crystal skulls 'talking' to each other when they are in each others presence - or even at a distance. Energy knows no bounds. Their original source is not of this Earth.

Old skulls are ones made centuries ago. These include the ones that are in many of the museums throughout the world. Most of these have been made by man, although there are some that contain no visible marks or evidence of modern tools upon them. These are the skulls that are typically thought of when one thinks of a crystal skull. They usually look human, and are often the size of a small human-sized skull. Most were under the care of a shaman, who would transmit the information from the skull to the people. Some old skulls are human skulls decorated with gemstones. The energy of these honored skulls are also palpable. Great care has gone in to their preservation and reverence throughout the ages.

Due to the intense energy surrounding

these skulls, they have been shrouded in mystery and fear. Skulls are seen as symbols of death in some cultures, so their elevated status confuses some. If it is realized that the brain, the seat of consciousness and understanding, is housed in the skull, then one begins to ascertain the importance of the skull as housing this important anatomical structure. Healers began to understand the vibrations that could be sensed through palpation of the skull, and may healing disciplines developed from that understanding. Cranial Osteopathy, also called Osteopathy in the Cranial Field, and its' offshoot, Cranial Sacral Therapy, are modern, as well as scientific modalities of this ancient practice. It is now well understood that energetic frequencies, wavelengths and electro magnetic transmissions all affect the brain, and thus the organism who's brain it is. These effects affect the mind, body and spirit of a person, and the health of the triune nature of the being.

Ancient skulls are those that have seeded this planet with their essence. Some are no longer in this dimension. There are ones who have been rumored to have inter-dimensional origins, such as the elusive Blue skull, which has made its presence known recently. Ancient skulls exhibit no evidence of machining. These ancient skulls came together to form a whole that was the template of love and peace - also the template of the skulls that were to be patterned after these in this dimension. Many of the 'old' skulls are patterned after these ancient ones. Most of these are no longer in this dimension, but may be called upon by those with the crystal guardian codes hidden (within the light codes of the DNA), especially in the presence of a fully activated crystal skull. As the DNA has been upgrading over the past few years, many have realized their connection to the crystal skulls, and have considered or have become - a crystal skull guardian. These are the 'people' who have their origins in the stars as well. The crystal skulls provide a medium for 'talking' with their star family for some star people.

As agents of change and peace, the skulls have an etheric link to each other, the multi-verse, and the star patterns of their origin. It is this origin that is also the beginning of the soul of man, thus the patterning of the consciousness is the same of the elevated light human of which we are evolving towards - homo luminous - the light human. It is the resetting of the next golden age. The last one was 26,000 years ago. The cycle has now come full circle as of December 21, 2012, and the newly emergent energies have now begun to bring this golden age into its' full fruition. It is the culmination of the prophesies during the 'dark ages' that the light has returned. It is now as a result of that return, that the skulls are speaking to those who have incarnated here at this time to participate in this process with them.

As humans begin to realize their origins from the stars, many are noticing changes within themselves. Some are even realizing they have an attraction to crystal skulls, and are now becoming crystal skull guardians. As the right frequency is encountered, the dormant ability becomes activated. Perhaps the stones are beginning to talk to you, or the animals, plants or sky? The world is energy. Some of this energy is condensed to form what is perceived as matter, but is in actuality light energy that vibrates in a manner to appear as form. Quantum physics and mysticism are revealing similar truths as their paths converge and the knowledge unfolds. How wonderful that we live in this time to rediscover the lost art of communication with beings from beyond the stars, and that we can come together to rebuild the age of light, love, harmony and peace.

This is the story of how the crystal skull from beyond the stars, StarChild, was brought into my life. She has been a guiding force for good not only in my life, but in many of the lives she has touched. This book contains the channelings that have come through her throughout the time period March 2012 to November 2013. You are welcome to follow her on Facebook 11 page (https://www.facebook.com/MysticStarChildCrystalSkull?ref=hl) and 'like' her to get her more recent channelings. I encourage you to explore your own relationship with the crystal skulls to see if you resonate with becoming a crystal skull guardian yourself.

The Crystal Skull Explorers, Joshua and Katrina, can help pair you with a loving Crystal Skull being that can help change your life, and this planet we live upon, as we come together in love, peace and harmony. They can be reached at

crystalskullexplorers@gmail.com.
StarChild Channelings:
https://www.facebook.com/MysticStarChildCrystalSkull?ref=hl

Table of Contents

Prologue...5

Introduction to the ET/StarChild Skull by crystal skull explorers, Joshua Shapiro and Katrina Head..15

StarChild the Beginning............................25

How to Use this Book................................55

The StarChild Channels............................59

Where do we go from here?....................309

Acknowledgements..................................315

Author's Bio...317

Bonus material:..319
Starkeepers channelled info

StarChild Photo Gallery..........................343

An Introduction to the ET/StarChild Skull, The King/Laialani

by the Crystal Skull Explorers, Joshua Shapiro and Katrina Head

Joshua: In 2010, Katrina and I were contacted by a production team in England that had been hired by National Geographic to do a show called The Truth About the Crystal Skulls.

We met them in at the end of January in 2011 at a Hotel in San Francisco, California, where I was interviewed for 3 hours.

They had behind me during the interview, an amazing human size clear quartz skull with a movable jaw that was done by a master carver in China. Although this crystal skull did not have much energy connected to it, the carving was very accurate.

A few weeks after the interview was over we asked the British Production Company if they could help us contact the carver, as they had gone to China to interview the owner of the Carver's company and the carver who made this wonderful clear quartz human-sized skull. But before I received word from the Production company I started speaking to a group selling crystal skulls on e-bay under the name Rikoo and discovered they were the carvers of the skull behind me for the interview and also knew about me as well due to this TV Show.

So indirectly, the British Production Company and National Geographic had brought us together with the Chinese Carvers who I started to speak to Rikoo's owner around April of 2011.

In 2011, Katrina and I were doing a lot of traveling in the U.S. and Canada sharing our public crystal skull events and in each place we go, a certain amount of the people want to buy their own crystal skulls so Rikoo helped us this year to offer people their skulls.

But Katrina and I were looking to offer some unique crystal skulls and we came up with the idea to see if Rikoo could make for us duplicates of two of our personal crystal skulls. One is our skull called "Geronimo Golden Eagle-Eye" which is a dark smoky quartz skull made by a well known Brazilian carver, which holds the energy and spiritual essence of the Indigenous cultures in our world. And the other skull was our Star Being Skull (The King / Laialani) which had been made by a Chinese carver and looks like an ET skull but we never found out (it was a secret) who this original carver was that had create the "Star Being" Skulls. Rikoo agreed to work with us for the Junior Skulls we called them - and we began work on them in June of 2011 and by August-September we had our first Junior Skulls to offer - which members of our Crystal Skull Newsletter first acquired and then we had more copies that traveled with us during the last quarter of 2011.

At the end of 2011, we setup a coast to coast tour which took us from the Seattle area, across the U.S. till we reached near

Ashland, North Carolina.

This tour was done by car and began on October 26th, 2011 and we returned to our home in Washington in early December of 2011, after stopping by Linda's home in southern Illinois. The first part of our tour took us through Washington, Oregon, Idaho, and Utah - we stopped and visited with friends near Salt Lake City. Then we traveled through Wyoming (where we saw many UFO clouds in the sky) and came to the Denver area where we visited with Friends.

Coincidentally as we were traveling East, Hunbatz Men, a Mayan Daykeeper who has his own ancient crystal skull had been traveling West, starting from New York City with a group of people, and stopping in Sacred Places along the way and doing ceremonies with crystal skulls so we were visiting a few places the same as we headed East and Hunbatz Men headed West. As we were headed toward our work in the St.Louis Area (a lecture, workshop and privated sessions) from Denver we met Hunbatz Men at his hotel in Hays, Kansas as he was headed next to Colorado. Hunbatz Men had just done a ceremony at the Cahokia Mounds in Southern, IL (many Indian mounds here) for which we were headed for the Star Knowledge Conference that was nearby after we finished in St.Louis.

Now how we came into contact with Linda was, just before we left for our coast-to-coast tour, Linda found us on the internet and had requested via an on-line form, our free crystal skull e-book. In our following interaction via email we found out that she lived in southern Illinois not too far from where we would be in the St.Louis area and then she also told us that like ourselves, she would have also have a booth at the Star Knowledge conference. Linda setup to do a private crystal skull session with us before the Star Knowledge Conference and this is how we first met Linda. Linda of course also had a chance to meet all of our crystal skulls and to see what crystal skulls we had that were looking for their new homes.

Katrina remembers that the new King / Laialani Jr. skulls for this tour did not come to our home in Seattle but were shipped to our sponsors home near St. Louis and arrived there from China before we came to

St.Louis. According to our records, Linda had her session with us on November 6th, 2011. It is here that she first saw "StarChild" and picked out the "StarChild" template from the Jrs. we had. The particular skull that Linda received was not given to her until the StarKnowledge Conference. It was at this conference that Linda asked us to hold this crystal skull for her, so "StarChild" could be charged more fully by our personal crystal skulls which we call our Crystal Children. The StarChild skull was also more fully charged with our crystal children about one month later when we spent a night at her home while she was still living in southern Illinois.

The Star Knowledge Conference is a conference that has been organized over many years since the early 1990s by Standing Elk, a Lakota Elder. The goal of the Star Knowledge Conference is to bring together Indigenous Spiritual Elders and Shaman to share their sacred teachings and prophecies along with other Spiritual Teachers of many different backgrounds. To the Native Americans, they know about the Star Elders (or ETs) and so UFOs is also a part of the conference. In the first Star Knowledge Conference offered in SD in the early 1990's, I attended to speak about the crystal skulls and was accompanied by Joky van Dieten who is the guardian of the ancient crystal skull called "ET" - which is a human size single piece of smoky quartz crystal that looks like an ET being. So it was about 20 years since Joshua had spoken about the crystal skulls at the Star Knowledge.

The King, the one who points the way (Masculine aspect)
Laialani (Feminine Aspects)

If you feel an affinity to Starchild and wish to get a skull like this
of your own in amethyst, Joshua and Katrina have contacted some
special carvers to do this - (we could send you a photo to include of
one if you want here) - just go to their webpage at:

http://www.v-j-enterprises.com/King-Laialani-StarBeingSkulls.htm
http://www.crystalskullexplorers.com

The King/Lialani skull - photo courtesy of the Crystal Skull Explorers

http://www.whatarecrystalskulls.com

Here is a description of this crystal skull:

The 'King' (The One who Points the way, or the masculine side name) or 'Laialani' (the feminine side name) is what is called a 'Star Being' skull and is less then 1 lb., made from amethyst quartz. Joshua has tried to discover who the carver is that is making these type of skulls (hundreds or thousands are being made) but all we know is that it is a Chinese carver. Some people feel the shape of this skull resembles the Gray Aliens somewhat but for us, this skull has never held such type of frequencies or energies.

Joshua received this crystal skull as a gift from Sharon White Elk Woman, from Kent in England, when he participated in the fall of 2008 in a Crystal Skull Conference (or 'Taster' as we called it) in Glastonbury in England. White Elk Woman told Joshua that a specific crystal skull had requested to go with him. The masculine name for the skull did not come until about 2 months later, when Joshua was visiting a friend in Los Angeles and did a meditation with the skull with music from his MP3 player, right before going to sleep. Here is what happened:

First Joshua felt to raise this skull in his left hand, high in the air above him and away from his body. Then he felt and saw (Joshua's gift of inner sight is not so strong), a powerful purple beam of light come from above him and cover his hand and arm, holding the skull. He felt a communication on a feeling level with dimensional beings. Then he heard, 'My name is The King, and I am the One who Points the Way' and he felt the 'King' literally moving him off in a direction, representing a direction of life he should travel.

In 2009, some people felt a more feminine aspect to this crystal skull and at a small presentation we gave in the Atlanta area, a good friend of Katrina's in attendance was holding this crystal skull and said the feminine side felt like 'Laialani,' a woman's name from Hawaii, so we decided to keep it. This skull works with people who are 'Star People' or 'ET Souls' and shows how such people are able to integrate their star-self with their human side. Katrina also feels (perhaps these were the dimensional beings who contacted Joshua) 'The King/Laialani' also is connected with the Hathors.

For more about the Crystal Skull Exployers, visit:
http://www.crystalskullexplorers.com
http://www.whatarecrystalskulls.com

StarChild - The Beginning

Crystal skulls have always held fascination for me. There was an inexplicable draw that overcame me when ever I saw a picture of one, or the subject was brought up. If I saw one in a museum, I would get messages from them. I just 'knew' their realm somehow.

While in medical school, I was in the student osteopathic club, and took a great interest in cranial osteopathy. It came natural to me, and I could feel the cranial rhythmic impulse immediately, even in a loud room of nearly 100 people. From there, I helped to bring great cranial osteopaths to my school, via the cranial academy, as vice president of the Undergraduate Association of Osteopathic medicine. For one of these events, I was to pick up the boxes of skulls, both articulated and whole and to keep them at my condominium until they were needed for the workshop. This gave me the rare opportunity to spend time alone with these incredible teaching tools full of life and presence. They spoke to me in terms of healing, and so much more. I could feel the inherent energy contained in these skulls. Their wisdom was palpable.

While I was studying cranial osteopathy, in addition to the rest of my studies, I began to immerse myself in the study of shamanism. Energy was my passion, and spirit had given me a mission for this lifetime, blending the differing disciplines into one holistic medium. The book, Mystic Awakening of an American Physician' tells this part of the story. A decade later, as a fully vested shamanic practitioner, and while immersing myself in cranial osteopathy and holistic medicine, spirit began to have me apprentice shamanic students.

The apprenticeship was intense. Three years of self discovery, journeying and learning to work with and master the energetic forces needed to transform the world and themselves. This involved a trip to the Amazon in Peru, as well as the sacred valley, to work with the most highly regarded shamans in the world, the elusive alto-misayo. These fine students were the cream of the crop, and all went on to become very highly regarded shamans in their own right, and still do the work as directed by Spirit.

On one of the long weekends, we met for an advanced shamanic class at a retreat center on the Ohio river. Perched high above the river, one could see for miles across into the Kentucky countryside, ablaze with the autumnal glory. The river mirrored the reds, oranges, yellows and pinks of the turning leaves. Barges were often seen transversing the waters below. This is a sacred place where miracles happen, and this particular weekend the weather reports were for severe weather, such as tornadoes, high winds and driving rains.

The subject for that weekend was crystalline structures, including water, crystals, and the life force. It was an incredible weekend with intense storms. Lightning flashed all around us as we honored the spirit of water, crystals and the crystalline structures that the water resonates with. We felt safe and protected even though lightning (and we would find out later - tornadoes) and thunder were all around, but we were held, safe in the sacred protection of the primal elements of life.

After we finished a ceremony outdoors to honor those powerful elements, we went indoors and began a meditation. The sounds of thunder was heard in the distance. Three large quartz crystals were in the middle of the circle. The energy was very powerful as the meditation began. All of a sudden, a silvery-gold shining disc-like being appeared above us. The being spoke with a deep loud voice, saying, "I am the carver of the crystal skulls!" and then a crystalline pyramidal vortex opened up around us, enveloping us within. Suddenly, 12 or 13 crystal skulls began flying in a large, clockwise, circle around us. The voice said the original skulls were being reunited and this is the key to usher in the age of enlightenment and peace. One was seen to be recovered in a high mountain as a glacier retreated, that was the last one to be revealed, the necessary one to reactive the circle to its full complement of power. It has a very primitive looking face, not the type one ordinarily thinks of when thinking of a crystal skull. The 'one' was to unite the remaining 12. It looked like a wagon wheel of crystal skulls circling above.

It was very clear that this was to be a part of my journey to integrate into my mission here. All of the participants saw the skulls and experienced this intense and extreme dimensional doorway open. It was an honor for all of us.

The next morning when we woke up and went outside, there were incredible whirls of what looked like roses make of frost. I had never seen anything like that - and it spoke to the beauty of the night before (we would find out that is a rare occasion when swirling winds freeze the dew called 'frost-flowers'). We continued to honor the element of the crystalline structure of life, including water (frozen and fluid) and crystals, as we headed home from the weekend. It was a truly magical.

After that weekend, the healings began to change. The being, the shining disc that said he had carved the crystal skulls, began to come in the rooms, wrapping the person in the crystal pyramid during the healing session. He said his name was 'Ahten' as best as can be said in English. Ancient Egyptian in nature, he began to show me certain things regarding skulls, harmonics, crystals, music, and how all were related to each other and to the person on the table, in particular. The vibrational constant indicated the frequency of the harmonic needed to heal the person according to their unique energy signature. Straightening out the 'dent' in the vibration led to them healing themselves. I was only a vessel for this energetic construct to occur through.

For the next two years I would occasionally have dreams about the skulls. One in particular would come to me in dreams. I would go to rock shops, but never saw any when I would look for them. I began to not even think too much about them after awhile.

Meanwhile, the date of November 11, 2011 was almost here. This number was a very significant one for me, and approaching fast. As a child, my Pleaidean star-being father would sit at the right side of my bed and talk to me and stroke my hair and face until I fell asleep. At around age eight or so, I began to notice the time 11:11, and then my star father would put his hand on my head and I would sleep. Eventually I just drew comfort from the stars when I saw the time 11:11. (he only rarely came once I approached adolescence). This number was given to me, as it had been given to so many others, for it was an awakening code. I had waited, along with many others for this incredible vibrational vortex to occur, and as it drew near, spirit said to me to 'go to Cahokia Mounds and meditate at 11:11 on 11-11-11.'

Cahokia Mounds is a sacred earthen mound ceremonial complex, where the star family of the bird people reside. There is a 'wood-henge' there, which marks the equinoxes and solstices. 'Munks Mound' is the largest earthen mound in the United

States, and was the ceremonial center of the Cahokia Mounds complex. This is located near St Louis, MO on the Illinois side of the MIssissippi River. It's location was about two hours north of my house at the time. I knew I was destined to go there on that sacred day.

I wrote on Facebook that I was instructed to go there, as per spirit's instructions. I asked if anyone wanted to go with me. A friend of mine wrote "don't you know there is a gathering there at that time?"

"No, I didn't know that," I said.

She said, "The Star Knowledge people were gathering over the weekend there at a local hotel." There would be speakers, meditations, The Crystal Skull explorers, Chiefs with Star Knowledge, seers, a Kahuna, and more.

This sounded exactly like something spirit would assign me to, so I called and made my reservations. I knew of no one from my local community who wanted to go with me, so I decided I would go and vend my first book 'Mystic Awakening of an American Physician,' spiritual art I painted, some Peruvian textiles, and an Amazon Jungle and Sacred Valley retreat I was to facilitate.

When I saw the list of speakers for this event, the names of the Crystal Skull Explorers, Joshua Shapiro and Katrina Head, gave me an intense vibe. I knew I needed to write them and to tell them of the experience I had at the retreat center a couple years prior. I didn't expect to hear back from them, as they travel extensively with their crystal 'children,' but I followed Sprit's advice and wrote them anyway.

This is the original email transmission, including mis-spellings. Please note www.drhostalek.com is no longer an active website. The current website is www.holisticwellnesshawaii.vpweb.com

You may, however, contact Joshua and Katrina at their email address and website below.

original email transactions:

To: Joshua Shapiro <crystalskullexplorers@gmail.com>
Cc: inka.princess1@gmail.com
From: Linda Hostalek <lindahostalek@me.com>
Subject: Re: hope you are enjoying the free e-book, events in St.L & IL
Date: Fri, 21 Oct 2011 06:05:46 +0000 (GMT)
X-Mailer: MobileMe Mail (1F25)
X-Originating-IP: [173.16.137.216]

Hi Joshua

Thank you for the nice email. I am looking forward to meeting you
and your skulls in Cahokia. (and getting that book!)
I am in Carbondale, IL in southern IL Where will you be in St
Loius? That is much closer to me that Champaign, I would be
interested to know more about your event there.

The first time I encountered crystal skulls was at the gold museum

in Lima, Peru
they were mostly partially crystal, but they began to talk. That
was after an incredible initiation on Macchu Pichu about 15years
ago. They have always intrigued me, but it was not a huge focus for
me at the time.
I always knew when the time was right, they would come into my life.

About 5 years ago it was time.

I was teaching my advanced shamanic apprentice students and we began
a meditation with some crystals (that had come into my possesion by
a man who stopped by my place a few years prior with several large
crystals, basically delivering them to my door. He was led to just
'stop by', and delivered several crystals that I didn't even know
that I was supposed to have, and left again, never to be seen or
heard from again. In any event, as I led this particular
meditation, these crystal wanted to be part

of it. Then, this
crystalline being came down out of the sky and began introducing
himself as "the carver of the crystal skulls". He dove down inside
the circle of light, illuminating it with several colors and
vibrations of love, light and healing that went into each of our
hearts, turning the circle into a pyramid. I was shown a variety of
skulls (about 12 -13) that have been and they began to dance around
our heads under a crystal pyramid. Each one began to tell about
its' self, each was a primal seed.
I was told that as they come together the 'next' begins
I was shown that there were some yet to be discovered, including one
that would be recovered from the retreating glacier in what appeared
to be siberia, and when they came together humanity would evolve
into the 'next'
i also saw 2 other skulls in particular being brought out of a dark
underground place, those both seemed of

mayan origin (it appeared to be a holy underground shamanic portal that it came out from, a human appearing hand retrieved it)
i have no confirmation if these skull have surfaced yet, this has been about 5 years, but I can feel their presence and it has grown increasingly stronger over the past few years especially, as humanity evolves and the skulls grow stronger, or perhaps as the skulls grow stronger, humanity evolves. It is activation of the DNA light codes.
since then, this being comes when I do healings on certain people we are put in a crystal pyramid and the healing begins. This will usually begin when I have my hands on a person's skull doing some cranial work (I am a cranial osteopath as well as a medical intuitive)
The being's name is (not sure how to spell) 'Ahten' and appears as a shiny disc of light from the apex of the crystal pyramid, occasionally taking a humanoid crystal

translucent male form, the voice is male
The skulls are all connected from an
extra-terrestial star source -
the star beings themselves
that is why some have no markings
lasers are also involved in their making
somehow
the one buried in the glacier seemed to be
the key to the awakening
of the others
I believe it has happened and that they are
talking and resonating
with each other bringing in the new 'next'
the Ahten is the one who gave the wisdom
to Egypt
and was incarnated at one time as the
pharoah, Ahknaten
Also was the star seed for all great cultures

I would be interested to hear your thought
on this. I am looking
forward to meeting your skulls next month.
Perhaps even in St
Louis, as that is much closer than
Champaign is for me, I live in
southern Illinois. About 2 hours south of
Cahokia. I had planned
to go to the mounds and meditate on

11-11-11, when I found out about the conference. The synchronicities are exciting, something wonderful is about to happen, and for me, when I saw that you will be there with your skulls, it seemed especially synchronistic.

As I looked at the pictures of the skulls, the one that resonated the most with me was the lemurian/et skull, not sure right now what the name is, but I hope to meet that one next month.

And yes, I am an 'Inka princess'. Perhaps that is why things talk to me (I wrote a book on that subject - Mystic Awakening of an American Physician). But that is a discussion for a different day.

Many blessings to you and your 'children' Looking forward to our paths crossings

Linda

Linda Hostalek, D.O.
Holistic Wellness Institute, Inc.
www.drhostalek.com
http://www.greatmystery.org/cmd.php?af=1395413
On Oct 20, 2011, at 09:12 AM, Joshua Shapiro <crystalskullexplorers@gmail.com> wrote:

Hi Linda

thanks you for your interest in our free e-book and we did get
your order for a copy of our 1st crystal skull book which hopefully
my father in Bloomington IL will send to you soon as we have
only a few copies left

oh I see you are coming to Cahokia - great - we will have
15 skulls to share and other skulls who are looking for
their new homes

if you are comfortable - we would be

interested to hear about
the information you channeled

also be aware from Nov. 4 - 6 we are in the St.Louis area,
but I think Carbondale is close to Champaign so it might
be a bit far to go - info about our events however is shown
at:
<http://www.v-j-enterprises.com/csevents.html>www.v-j-enterprises.com/csevents.html

see you in November, thank you Linda

Joshua & Katrina
the crystal skull explorers

PS - to sign up for our free online newsletter, go to:
<http://www.whoisjoshuashapiro.com/newsltter-signup.htm>www.whoisjoshuashapiro.com/newsltter-signup.htm

were you an Inka Princess before?

>person_name: Linda Hostalek
>
>organization: Dr Linda Hostalek, Inc/Holistic Wellness Institute
>
>email_name: <mailto:inka.princess1@gmail.com>inka.princess1@gmail.com
>
>city: Carbondale
>
>state: IL
>
>country: United States
>
>comments: About 5 years ago, I channeled a being who told me he was
>the carver of the crystal skulls, and showed me some phenomenal
>things. The presence of many crystal skulls came that day, and that
>star being in still in constant contact. I am very interested in
>learning more about your skulls that you are caretakers of, and to
>hopefully be able to have some time with the skull being
>itself. Thank you so much for making this

available. I look
>forward to meeting with you in Cahokia
>
>CSE_Print: ON

To my surprise, he wrote back the very same day, and was interested in learning more abut my experience. Both Joshua and Katrina are extremely psychic, and they picked something up about me and crystal skulls that I did not fully appreciate at the time.

It turned out they were having a workshop in St Louis that weekend, and asked if I would come up and meet with them as their guest. They reserved a room for me, and I made the two and a half hour trip to meet with them and their group.

It was a rainy dark evening, in early November. Due to construction and GPS taking me to roads that were now closed, I was too late for the evening workshop, but met with them over dinner at a local italian restaurant. We had a wonderful time and realized we had spent lifetimes before doing this work. We decided we would have a session with their skulls the next day, and we parted ways until then.

As I lay in my bed that night, a large, crystal skull appeared over my bed and stood guard over me all night long. I knew this skull, I had spent lifetimes with it, and it was very familiar to me. I slept soundly in the cabin, just me, my dog, Lotus, and this lovely wonderful skull levitating over me.

The next day when I met with Joshua and Katrina, they had an array of skulls on the table. They had just acquired a beautiful new rose quartz skull, Rosalita, and she was in the middle behind a powerful clear crystal skull. They had asked that no one touch Rosalita, as her energy was extremely high, as she carried the vibrations of multiple dimension and lifetimes. She had a detachable jaw and also carried energy of the cosmos. Their other skull children, Portal, Geronimo, the ET star being skull, The King/Laialani, and several others where also on the table holding space for what promised to be an interesting encounter.

As space was opened and we began to enter inter-dimensional space-time, I was attracted to the large rose quartz skull, Rosalita, Portal de Luz, and also the star being skull King/Laialani.

Then, Joshua and Katrina both looked at each other, then at me, then at each other and they said "Rosalita wants you to hold her" to me. I was stunned and honored that this magnificent being would choose me to hold her. They told me I was to exchange energies with her.

As they placed her in my lap - I instantly went to this beautiful blue place of my origin. I was no longer on Earth. I saw the beings that I have encountered since childhood, and recognized this blue world with the tall, transparent, blue light beings. I also recognized Joshua and Katrina from there, and many other inter-dimensional attributes came through. It was extremely beautiful, and I am forever grateful for that encounter. Joshua confirmed that I came from the blue field from beyond the Pleiades, that the Pleiadean-ness was a step-down energy for my vibration so that it could have form. There were also remnants of Andromeda, Lyria, the bird people, and a few other places as well. He also told me that in a past life, I had been a crystal skull guardian, and that energy was calling me back to this profound relationship with the skulls. I then saw the skull that had been levitating over my bed. We have had lifetimes together.

Joshua is my brother, and we have spent many lifetimes together. Katrina is my sis*star, and her and I are linked throughout time as well. I came home to family that day, and my life has been forever enriched.

Their skull children all had their part to play, and I knew that the ET/star being skull, The King/Laialani was the type I was to be the guardian of. They had some crystal skull 'children' waiting to be adopted, but none of them resonated with me in that particular way. They informed me that their carvers were shipping out some more and they would have them when they came to Cahokia on November 11. I knew the being that would be coming into my life would be coming through that channel. And so I left it at that, and agreed to pick her up when we met again in Cahokia.

Later that same week, after that incredible weekend, I received an email about Hubatz men, and his tribe of crystal skull guardians that were activating sacred spots from coast to coast. They began on the east coast, Serpent Mound, and would be at Cahokia Mounds prior to continuing their journey west to California, where they would be on November 11, 2011. Again, I had that knowing that I needed to go. This time, two of my shaman friends joined me. We went to the mound and did ceremony to activate and energize the area for the ceremony that would be taking place for the crystal skulls. Spirit directed us to a place on the mounds, and we put our love and essences in to the spot with the intention of good will, love and harmony for this future age that was unfolding, and the ceremony that would be happening here later.

In the morning, a workshop was held prior to the ceremony. There were so many people that the meeting place needed to be changed to handle the crowd. They each introduced the different skulls that had made this incredible journey and the energy was palpable. When the elder, Hunbatz man, was talking, he spoke of an ancient skull gifted to him by a Himalayan Shaman for this journey of activation. When he held up the skull for all to see, its essence permeated my very being - this was the same skull that was shown to me by the silvery gold shining disk being who called himself 'the carver of the crystal skulls' years ago! I saw that skull being revealed by the retreating glacier, fulfilling the prophesy of its essence required to bring in this new age of light. I was God-smacked.

We then returned to the mound to await Hunbatz man and his group. I was drawn to a spot on the mound, and stayed on that spot, connecting with the vibration. This was not the same spot we had held ceremony, but nearby, and I just knew I needed to 'be there.'

The crowd was a younger crowd than one usually sees at such a gathering, although people of all ages were present. There were babies, children, young adults, middle age and even the elderly. The energy was that of a torch passing from one generation to another. These young people were expecting to live their lives in a different fashion than that of previous generations, and to bring their children up with that intention. That was exciting to witness. One could feel the wheels of history changing. The new age was beginning, and this was part of the transition. The torch was being passed as it lit up this new age of love and light. This was part of the transition of the rapidly approaching 11-11-11 vortex.

I was still standing and being present with that spot on the mound. Most were near the stairs awaiting Hunbatz man and his group to climb up to the top of the mound. When they made it up the stairs, He came right up to me, and motioned for me to move from where I had been holding space, and he put his skull on the spot I had been holding space on. The other skulls were arranged, and then the people were arranged for the ceremony to begin. He motioned for me to be one of those participating in the ceremony. I was a moon.

As we began, the connection was made, and those of us appointed to be there did our part in this ceremony of transition. I can still feel the echoes of this ceremony in my soul.

The next week or so, it was November 11th. I connected with the Crystal Skull Explorers, Joshua and Katrina, and was ready to connect with the skull that I would be responsible for. They had received a new box of similar skulls from the skilledChinese carvers, and they were still in the box. I could feel the energy and knew exactly which one it was. Katrina asked me "Do you want to see them first?"

I said "OK, but I already know it is this one here," as I pointed to one of the skulls in the box. As she took the skulls out one by one, they were all beautiful and had wonderful energy, but I knew the one in the particular position in the box was the one. When she pulled her out, I knew why. A lovely, lavender purple beauty, she embodied the stars in her being. We were finally reunited!

She told me her name was 'StarChild,' and she began to talk. She wanted to spend some time with her brother and sisters, Geronimo, Portal de Luz and Rosalita, to transfer information between them. One could see the energy transfer happen as the downloading began. The next couple of nights they connected, and she began to go with me nearly everywhere. The incredible 11-11-11 mediation at both 11:11 am and pm were extraordinary, and she was part of them both.

The morning meditation connected all of us together throughout all the differing dimensions, and through out space-time, marking this spot on the transition of the ages. The evening meditation, sent me on my star parents' Pleiadean space ship, crowning me with a blue, purple and white light, and a knowing ness that it was now time to teach the space medicine. From that point on, the tones out of my mouth changed, and my healings took on a very different turn (they continued to be incased in a crystal pyramidal vortex). Star beings would routinely show up and do the healings or show me what was needed for that person. I began to make new sounds, and I began to communicate in earnest with StarChild. She would talk to me everyday.

The channelings became daily events that would set the tone for the day. I was amazed at her clarity and accuracy about what was to come. She became a trusted guide, and would often channeling information or healing for others as well.

A couple of months later, while co-facilitating a women's retreat with my dear friend, Pamela Panneton of Land Spirits, StarChild began to share her information with the group. The first night she wanted to sleep with Pamela, and she kept her up all night long talking to her. They have been close friends ever since. One night we had a party where we wore stick-on jeweled bindis and she wanted one too! That is how she got her beautiful blue bindi on her third eye. She participated in all of this, doing readings and healings, and then, near the end of the retreat she made an announcement. "I want my own

Facebook page," she went on, "so I can communicate with the world.' How could I refuse? The information channeled through her has helped others, and many have written me to tell of how she has helped them. Many ask about her story as well as how to obtain a collection of her channels. That is how this all began, and how this book came to be. It has been a profound honor to receive the channels through StarChild. Thank you for coming along on this fabulous journey. Bless.
https://www.facebook.com/MysticStarChildCrystalSkull?ref=hl

StarChild at the retreat in Ocean City, MD the day she requested her Facebook page. February 2012 with Pamela Panneton of Land Spirits
www.landspirits.com

If you feel an affinity to Starchild and wish to get a skull like this
of your own in amethyst, Joshua and Katrina have contacted some
special carvers to do this - (we could send you a photo to include of
one if you want here) - just go to their webpage at:

http://www.v-j-enterprises.com/King-Laialani-StarBeingSkulls.htm

How to Use this Book

These channelings contain the energy of a particular time and/or day. As you pick up the book, ask the universe to guide you to what you need for that time period, then find the page that 'calls' to you. You may find that a certain page or theme comes up for a while, then the energy changes and another theme emerges. It is all energy and as such, will pick up what your energy has to say and pair it with the proper page. Be mindful when doing this, and always remember to thank your guides and organizing principles of the Divine each day.

Remember that energy cycles, and as such, a reading that was written in the past can have the same vibrational essence as you are experiencing now. Trust and listen within yourself to decipher if this is true for you.

Some are very short, while others are

relatively long. No two are alike. When a channel is re-read, a different interpretation may occur.

StarChild has a way of reaching through space and time to tap in to what is the essence of the day. You may also just read through the channelings until you find one that speaks to you. If you are the guardian of a crystal skull, you may place your skull upon the book with your intent, and the energy of StarChild will inform the other crystal skull. She has a great desire to share her information with the world, and with other crystalline beings. You may be surprised by what your skull begins to transmit after that! Remember too, that StarChild will also become informed of the knowledge contained in the skull you are guardian of, for energy flows both ways. This way the energy is transmitted and the love ripples throughout the multiverse in a cosmic reunion of love, light, harmony and peace.

May you be blessed as you read these pages and integrate the vibration into your life. She has come from the stars to bring messages of hope, love and peace. By all of us growing in love and spirituality, may we increase the vibration of love and peace on this planet and bring about the golden age of peace and love. bless

The StarChild Channelings

These are the original readings, misprints and all, according to the day they were channeled. Know that energy is cyclical and as such, the vibrations come around in multiple forms. May these readings bless you as you resonate with the star energy it contains. bless

'The vortex that created this latest awakening has crested. This allows one to integrate that which is in their hearts and now. It is time to integrate that energy completely into your field. Resonate with this new found energy, as it is bonding and merging with your field. These next two weeks will allow you to see how this new awareness permeates most elements of your being. Take this time to let this settle into your field. Begin to think if there is another aspect of your reality you are aspiring to. If so, begin to ask the questions of yourself as to how to proceed. Your star family will be there to help see you through, but it is up to you to carry this forth. Know that they are watching over you and enabling you to proceed more clearly. Center yourself within the geometry of life, and follow the energetic lines to the next step. Remember to go to the stars at night and resonate with your star family. The connection will make the way clearer and enable one to follow the true path of light, love and peace.'-StarChild
11-15-13

'The vortex is now open and the next phase of expanding the potential of all is now here. It is time to grow and stretch beyond what you have thought you are capable of, and to bring in this new level of understanding. Continue to notice the geometry of the natural world, for it will enable you to resonate with the creative force which is growing strong within you. We have coded you with the song of the stars. Go to the evening sky and look to the south. See the patterns the stars have to show you. Bring that pattern into your field and receive the message. For the next three nights do this and your message will come through. The fabric of time has been altered, it is the new way of being. Be love, light, compassion, and happiness. It is time.'-StarChild
11-14-13

'Know that the sacredness of all creation is contained within. Look to the night sky and vibrate to the element of the stars, that is your true essence, and one that will lead you home. The vortex has opened to allow the secrets to be shown to you more easily. The secret is love, and that is what you are also made of. You come from the stars, and your vibration is known. Be pure, be true, and be the light you wish you see in this world. Your actions affect all as your essence permeates through the ether. Know you are sacred, as is all creation. Go within and see.'-StarChild
11-13-13

'Blessings abound on this most auspicious day of sacred numbers, shapes and colors. This vortex will continue as you embrace the consciousness within. Know your star family is present and is here to help, you have only to call and listen for the response. Be still and listen, and your answers will come.'-StarChild 11-12-13

'The spirals that one sees in all of nature connect all to all, From the nautilus shell to the shape of galaxies, know that you, too, are a part of this great continuum. Honor your place in the great cosmos, and know that you are as important as everything else. Your love, your involvement, and the energy you contribute all matter. We see you vibrating higher and higher as the consciousness of all beings is rising, Some are having trouble adjusting to the new way of being, but all are evolving one way or another. Change is the constant, and this is happening now. We are revealing ourselves to you in multiple ways to assure you the path you are taking is the right one. Look for us in the night sky in the north west, and see if you see our triangular ships and the orbs of blue and white light. We are here, and we are proud of the way you are evolving and adjusting to this new way of being. Look to the skies, and the know you belong, for all are connected in the great web of life and love.'-StarChild 11-8-13

'The patterns of sacredness are all around. One can observe this in the spirals of the galaxies, the whirls of hair on a baby's head or the microtubules of a microscopic organism. The patterns repeat to show that all is related, no matter how distant it may seem on the surface. All is important in the great scheme of breathe and life, as the cosmos breathes to the rhythm of life. This is true on this planet-being, Earth, as on the other planet beings. Next time you pick a flower and see a pattern within the seed head, know that is spirit revealing to you a secret of the multi-verse. Meditate upon that design of life, and know that pattern lives in you, growing, evolving and being love in a physical form. All is love, including you. Go vibrate your pattern of beauty to all today.'-StarChild
11-7-13

'You need not wait, only do. You have all you need to begin that which you have been contemplating. The time is now. Over time it may take a different form than it currently has, but by beginning now, you bring in the energy to hone this project as you see it in your field. You know what you need to do, it is now time to do it. Be in the vibration of love as you begin or continue this element of your field. It is your gift to the world when you act in this way, for others will respond to that which you create. If you put the vibration of love in to all that you do - it will help continue to shift the multiverse to the loving vessel of peace that it is to be. Do your part and love that which you are about to do. It is time - and it is good.'-StarChild
10-29-13

'There are choices all around you. The time is now to feel what is best for your incarnation here at this time. There are options all around you at this time. The energies have been focused on creating your full potential which is coming together now. This requires faith, courage and trust. Use this period of time to research your options and inner reflection. Weigh all your options carefully. Some things being put before you may seem good on the surface, but the structure is not secure - others may not look as pleasing, but have a better long term outlook for your quest at this time. That is why you must look carefully, feel the energy, and decide what your choice is, and be secure in your decision making. It is exciting as the energies you have been working so hard towards are finally beginning to manifest. Do not let fear dictate your choice, but rather consult with the divine in love and joy to allow the procedures to occur for the highest good of all concerned. By being true to yourself you allow the energies to coalesce from those streams of manifestation you have

been creating. Enjoy this time, be thankful for the gifts that are coming through, and even though this may mean a change in your situation, know that all is in divine right order. Choose from the place of love, peace and prayer, and trust that you are making the right choice. After all, you are choosing to participate in this co-creative process of making a life, and this is what you have planned on doing since your incarnation here. Welcome the new opportunities! Be smart, be true, and be conscious. Your choices carry great weight - but they need not be heavy. You know what you want. It is now time to go for it.'- StarChild
10-21-13

'Symbols are all around you, connecting you to your Star family above. They have been placed in holy places, in nature, and even in your bodies. Some will see these in visions, some in dreams, but each is a gift to direct you to the stars, and to the inner knowings of the mysteries of life. Triangles, spheres, rings, spirals, are all sacred symbols that transcend the mathematics of their existence. Know that as you meditate on those symbols that call to you, you are guided to the particular star gate that this symbol reveals. There are forms of the energy encoded in these sacred symbols, and many sites contain them. What do they mean to you? What symbols, shapes, colors or more speak to your heart and take you to another dimension? It is time to notice these, if you have not already, and take to heart the intense dimensionality that these symbols convey. You are love, are loved, have been loved, and will always be love. Love is the great connector, healer, manifestor, and more. By being in the vibration of the

essence of love that speaks to you, your personal vibration of the aspect of love you are charged with bringing to this planet will shine through. Bless the world with your love today.'-StarChild
10-14-13

'There are multiple star gates on this planet that you have access to. Holy places, designed to be energetically distinct from the area around it, have qualities that allow one to make contact with one's star family. This is but one of the ways in which we communicate with those on this planet. There is also a star gate built within your physical structure to communicate with your family from the stars. This is located in the third eye. Many of these star gates have already been awakened, and if you are now receiving messages, becoming more intuitive, or learning more about who you really are, the chances are that your personal star gate has been activated. You are here to resonate with the portals that are on this planet, with that which is within you, and to have communion with the star beings that are your family. This activation all over this world is very important to the rest of the multiverse, as this activation has implications beyond this small blue planet. Being from all over have made this blue planet being, Earth, a priority, for those who live amongst her are already taking their place in their stewardship of this great being. Love is the great healing force, and by activating the vibration of love within you, the resonance is amplified. The star gates are present to allow communication and energy to flow back and forth, healing this being and balancing the forces throughout the multi-verse. You are critical in this act, for your willingness to incarnate here and bring this vibration of love and healing to this planet being, Earth, and her inhabitants is what brings in the prophesies of the golden age that were foretold long ago, perhaps by some of you who had been here in a previous life. The attributes of love, peace, healing, and compassion bring in the knowingness that all is connected and each has a part to play. Honor your personal star gate within, as well as those distributed all over this planet, for by honoring this communication portal, this aspect of higher dimensional healing is available for all throughout the cosmos. Love, trust and appreciation are fuel to this process. You are here, and you are ready. We honor you for the work that you are doing, and are here to guide you, through the portals of the star gates, to help you complete your mission that you have incarnated here to do. Blessings of love, light and peace to you as you accomplish this great and mighty task.'-StarChild 10-11-13

'Know you are perfect just the way you are. The light you carry within you shines and enables the gift you bring to the multiverse to surface. Some shine softly, some quieter, but all shine in the vibration that is the perfect compliment to their vibration. The essence of love that permeates all beings, comes together to shift the vibration for the benefit of all. Continue to bask in the light of pure holiness, for that is your essence, and by just being you, you bring light. It is this light and love that changes the world and brings peace. Make peace your goal. It is coming.'-StarChild 10-5-13

'Little by little – that which you have been working towards is coming in to view. Know that you are where you are to be, for it is here that you are able to vibrate to your highest essence. Priorities are becoming known, and as that is revealed, you will find your essence is streamlined and more effective with less distraction. Continue to pray, meditate and be one with the joy of your soul. Know that you are loved and have the support of your star family. Begin to look to northern skies for the next several days – we will make ourselves known to you there. Be in the vibration of yellow, and remember to find the joy. Burn the essence of sage as you clean your space – inner and outer – to purify yourself for the next level of awakening. Be mindful and full of love, for good things are coming. You are ready.'–StarChild
10-4-13

'Today is a good day to clean up your space. This allows energy to flow and removes blockages while allowing opportunities to flow. You are an energetic mirror of your surroundings, and by clearing and cleansing your space, you are clearing yourself. Be in balance, in light and love, and flow in to the next. Fluidity allows connectivity, which allows fruition. Be mindful and clear and allow the blessings to flow.'-StarChild
9-27-13

'Balance is the key principle in all relationships. There is balance between the light and dark cycles, the order of the planets in relationship to their orbiting star, the seasons, and in the relationships between humans and their environment. When balance is in place, the natural order takes place. This does necessarily mean that everything is exactly half and half all the time, but rather the overall balance is achieved. This allows a tension to occur that keeps the drive of creation in place. One breathes in and then breathes out to allow the function of breathing to occur. This releases that which is no longer needed and allows for the fresh input of new inspiration. Today the call is to seek balance. All have male and female energies, and together they make the great the whole. Movement and motion, are balanced with stillness, and both are required, for without both, creation stops. Where are you on your cycle? Dark? LIght? In? Out? Movement? Still? It matters not where you are at, only that the cycle continues for one to be at their best, in accordance with their vibrational essence. Honor your essence, and create from the light, but remember to retreat into the void for the ideas to germinate and manifest from there. You are exactly where you are meant to be, and going towards that which you are continuously creating. Be mindful as you do so, and you will find the process rewarding. Listen to your internal compass which directs you to do that which is in your vibrational field of love, for that is how you bless the world with your gifts! Honor your gifts and allow them to shine through. That is what makes you a unique vibration of the whole. All parts are needed, and you are no exception. You came to this world to create and maintain love. That requires the balance of also taking care of yourself. The relationship with self allows for one to come forth for others to be blessed by. Honor yourself, your love, and your gifts. You came here to share them with the world. Be mindful and be balanced. That is the way.'-StarChild 9-25-13

'Be in the flow. Allow yourself to just 'be.' That is who you are at your essence. That is beauty, joy, love and harmony, unimpeded by blockages, living in the flow.'-StarChild 9-14-13

'Where there is love, there is also hope. Both are supreme vibrations of healing that can set things right. As one remains in the harmonic of love, anything is possible, no matter how improbable. This is the realm of miracles, and they happen every day, all over this blue globe. You can call in your own miracle when the desire of your heart is pure, and you are in correct vibration with that being desired. You are called to a higher order, and during this time of manifestation of the evolutionary process of ascension, your DNA upgrade is now complete. Thus your desires now have a more altruistic thrust to them; that is by design. You are learning that all beings are one, and what affects one affects the others too. To see this you have only to look at your spirit vehicle of the human body. Made up of trillions of 'individual' cells, the organism is greatly affected if one of those cells goes against the good of the organism. Together, you can walk, talk, run, swim, dance, pray and much, much more. How you go about this is up to you,

but as you consider the whole in relationship to the one, you can see that what is good for all is good for the one, for the one is the whole, and vice versa. The love and healing you put forth in your vibrations affect more than just one being. That love combines with the love brought forth by others to manifest a larger, more productive love that heals all in the path. As this path is consciously directed, all can be healed through that unconditional love that shapes this multiverse into being. Realize that your thoughts matter, and remember to think healthy thoughts. Soon that which you have thought about will begin to change. Life is ever changing and malleable, you must decide which shape it will have. And that requires love and hope.'-StarChild
9-11-13

'The energies you are putting forth are noticed and are affecting the manifestations that occur on your planet-being, Earth. Continue to hold her in love, be kind to each other and pray for peace. All is going towards balance, remember this in your own life as well. When the balance is achieved, all is in harmony. Keep working towards the balance in your inner life, for that reflects the outward world too. Both are mirrors, and it is time to clean the mirror and understand your true reflection. You have been called to incarnate to this planet to be an ambassador for the new way of love, light, harmony and balance. Vibrate to those ideals of love and light and know that we are here to help you. Stay strong and remain true to the ideals of love and purpose. Look to the southern sky at twilight and find us there. We love you.'-StarChild
9-10-13

'Know that your thoughts matter. Every thought you think carries an energetic quanta that is part of the collective whole. When those thoughts are unified in a field of love, peace, harmony, kindness, and light; those forces become the dominating force that shapes this part of the multiverse. When one is mired in the despair and fear, the energy contracts, and the momentum slows. We are here to help you remember how powerful your thoughts are! Your loving energy carries healing vibrations which can change the way that life on this planet is immersed in.   Be in kindness, hope and love, for although sabers are rattling, they can be only noise if the power of love drowns out the sound and replaces it with the harmonics of love and peace. Be proactive in voicing that which you intend to manifest - for that is how manifestations occur. When all pull together the same way, the combined force is much greater than when pushed against each other. Join the intergalactic community in the quest for peace, and it shall happen eventually.

Remember you are responsible for your own energy field. Keep the love and peace, and know that we are here to support you in this endeavor. We have been meeting regularly just off planet and are monitoring what is done here on this planet-being, Earth. Her well being, and yours, are very important to us. We are all connected and what affects one affects all. Some of you will see us in the northern sky tonight. Bring your joy, light and love to all situations, and remember how powerful your thoughts can be. You are made of stars and as such, made of light. Bring your light to this situation and be the example of peace.'-StarChild
9-7-13

'We are here and watching over the energies that shape the future of this planet-being Earth. From the ways of those who have used her resources without regard to her need for balance and replenishing, to those who would impose their ways upon others, we have come to assist in the resetting of these energetic thought forms. Love, kindness, compassion and harmony is what is to shape this world. The balance needs to be restored and we are here to help in that restoration. Beings from galaxies far away have joined those who regularly watch over this planet to help shift the elements of fear to the vibration of love. Light and love are being poured into the hearts of those who are in the darkest of fears. Transformation is occurring. Each one is responsible for the actions of one's heart. Be in strength, love and courage during this period of change. The energies come together to shift the outcome as the collective manifestation occurs through collaborative love. Be a part of this manifestation of love. It occurs in small ways. Be kind to all you encounter today. It matters not what has happened in the past, today be kind and full of love, compassion, and healing. Forgive others or yourself if needed, and go forward in the courage. The energy is heavy, so therefore make your heart as light as you are able to to counter the fear and negativity out there. Many are acting out. Remember your thoughts matter greatly, and carry more weight than one probably is aware of. Therefore, be of a high vibration that all is being carried out according to the plan you created when you incarnated here on this planet-being. All is in Divine right timing. Love this planet being and all the inhabitants upon her, even those whose actions you do not condone. Love is multi-dimensional, and as such, is powerful beyond comprehension. The limited view upon the Earth is just a slice of the entire picture, and as you channel the light and love as you are able, not only will you enable your life here on Earth to transform, but the power of all together channeling the love that surpasses understanding, changes the multiverse and ushers in the golden age which is your purpose here along with the others who have chosen this

as their mission upon the earth at this time. Remember that you, too, come fro the stars, and will return there one day.
You are given the go ahead to manifest that which is in the best interest for all concerned. Spend time in prayer and meditation today and contemplate what this world looks like with peace. See it in your mind's eye and know that it is not only possible, but through the like minded intentions though out the multiverse, this will become a reality. Do not be distracted by the loud noises of posturing through the media outlets. Listen to your hearts, and know the changes you must do for peace in your life. Begin in your own home. Forgiveness, if needed, then love and compassion to all. You are here to make this world a better place. That comes from a place of love. Remember that you are love. Therefore, all you need to do is to be yourself. Share this love with the multiverse as we enter this new phase here. Intend peace. Notice your abilities are heightening. Healing gifts are now being increased, this is so that you may serve the Divine more powerfully through healing. Love and healing, beauty and joy,

remember this only, for that is real. The illusions that one must pass to get to this point are but way showers on the path. You are love. Be it.'-StarChild
9-5-13

'This time of great contrasts opens the way to look past the distractions and to look to the energetic root of the matter. Remember to always make peace your goal. Love, kindness and harmony will change the world, but doing the same old thing out of insecurity will not. Be strong but not arrogant, loving without being a doormat and kind without being taken advantage of. Boundaries are important for you knowing where you stand and what is important to you. Doing for own purpose of light and love is very important, for that fuels the love that is the birthright of all. However, remember to be open to the flow of change, love, and mystery as it unfolds along your path. Great changes are coming, and as each one brings the light they carry to the situation at hand, the manifestation of love powers the vibrational shift. Many of you have had decisions to make over the past few days of energetic discord. Do not change your mind now that the chaos has quieted down. Be strong and do what you know you must do, for it is written in your soul to do these things that elevate the vibration of all. Listen to the small still voice inside and know that love is the most powerful force there is. We come in peace, love and harmony to show you the same. You know where you are to go, and what you are to do, even if only in a slight direction. As you follow that direction, the way becomes clearer, and your intent more focused. Be in your power and love, for that is how the world is changed. Listen to the underlying energy, not the distractional shouts. Be still and keep your eyes to the skies. We are here and we are watching. Some of you will see us tonight in the southwest sky, some will see us in the north, but the shift will be felt if one tunes in this evening. Feel the love and shift the vibration to one of peace. That is your mission here.'-StarChild 9-2-13

'Large contrasts are being shown to you today for you to best determine what it is that you wish to manifest. Remember to seek harmony and peace through the vibration of love. Know you will make the best decision. Have courage and strength. Listen to the small still voice within – your star voice which guides you to the vibration that is in alignment with your soul's true purpose. Call in that which is for the highest good, and remember that your decision affects all – for all are connected and all are one. Know that large contrasts make the vibrational canvas large enough to see the subtle essences of what it is you are creating, so that you may manifest more clearly. Once you decide, own your decision and produce it in love. Many are being asked to evaluate that which they wish to create in this present dimension of time. You are as well. Do your creations align with your core essence? Does the energy around them feel purposeful and full of love? Is this the highest good for all beings? The

contrasts will show you the answers. Look to the sky, open your heart and seek our advice. Notice the subtle ways you are answered. We know what you are going through. That is why we are here, and are making ourselves present. Go in love, light and harmony, for that is always the right way.'- StarChild
8-30-13

'Sometimes that which you have put your energy into comes crashing through to fruition, almost surprising one in the intensity and speed. Continue to hold the vibration of love, peace and compassion as you manifest your life. Even when it seems that things are not working, know that the energy always works and the result will come eventually. There are some among you today who are beginning to doubt, and that doubt collapses the bubble of energy that you have just created When you are in love, faith, courage, strength, love and alignment with your soul's purpose, the way is made for you to experience that which is dearest to your heart. It is the way of manifestation and the law of attraction, which is the law of the multiverse. Know that what you seek you shall eventually find as long as you continue to be in the vibration of creation, light and love. Stay steadfast, and know that you are being guided by your star family to complete your mission that you incarnated here to do. You have help and support in this regard. Know you are a child of the light, and as such, the guidance you receive is to help not only you, but others as well, to make your way in this multiverse. Know that as you keep focused on the positive vibration of change, that change will come, do not be distracted by the loud noises that try to prevent you from focusing and attending to your mission. Keep your eyes to the skies, for much is happening in all the realms. Your prayers, energy and intentions are also noted and do channel the vibration in the way people come together and vibrate. Your thoughts are very important, as they create a field that creates matter to form in the way of intention. Be in love, strength and courage, and know that you are in the right place at the right time doing the right thing. It is your mission, and it is good.'-StarChild

'Take note of where you are right now. Notice the position of your body, the temperature, the smells, the lighting, the sounds, and any other pertinent details. Be immersed in this present moment and notice the landmarks around you. Focus on the now. Integrate into this reality, and be present. This enables one to hear the voices of one's star family more easily, without distractions of the future or the past. Those are only illusions, and time truly has no meaning other than in this earthy dimension. Be in the now, and from here, feel the direction of where you are going. Does it feel in correct vibrational alignment for your soul? Or does it pull to the left or the right? Are you on center? All of these are informational channels for you to discern. By using your discernment you will arrive at the exact spot you need to be to further your path. The fuel for this path is love, and remember the kindness as well. This world is moving towards one where there will eventually

be no war and no injustices. This world still has remnants of the contrast phase of showing what is unacceptable. Focus your energies, not on what is not in alignment with your vibration, but rather what it is you would like to see take its place. Focus on the love, kindness and harmony of all peoples, nations, races, and dimensions. All are connected and through that connection the tug of war of how to go forth is in full play. Tug on the side of light and love, for your prayers and voice matter. We are here and are showing ourselves to those who need to see us. Continue to keep your eyes to the skies and your hearts in the vibration of love, light, compassion and peace. Your love matters.'-StarChild
8-27-13

'Health is a gift you give yourself. Take the time today to recharge yourself, for there is still much work to be done. Fortify yourself for this mission, by taking this day to rest and relax. Make the time to connect with the natural world around you, for that nurtures your soul and gives peace to your body, by harmonizing the vibrational forces within and around you. Allow any densities to be released, so that you are a pure channel of light and love, which is your true essence. You will then find that you are in the best place to complete your mission you came here to do. Kindness, compassion, harmony, and love as required as you work for the peace between all. Make peace your goal within yourself as well, for then you are better equipped to deal with the things that are coming. We are here to remind you of your perfection in being, that you are exactly where you are supposed to be at this time. Take this day to take a pause and reflect, so you may direct your energies to that

which you came here for. Enjoy your gifts, your talents and those whom you love. The crystal being of rose quartz is one to surround yourself with today if possible. Channel the gentle love for self, others, and the multi-verse, as you connect to the vibration of health and wellness for all through the rose quartz. Connect to the color if you are not around the stone. It is good, and it is time.'-StarChild
8-25-13

'Unfulfilled expectation lead to much inner turmoil, best to allow the now to flow without expectations. Expectations often block the flow of what one wishes to create, by putting a 'stop' on the flow. Be open, be full of light and love, and watch as your life flows with the magic and majesty assigned to you. You created your life before you incarnated here – and we are here to remind you of that. This is not your first time here. We come in the skies to remind you of who you are and where you come from. Allow the manifestations to flow from the seat of love. Amazing results will follow.'-StarChild
8-23-13

'Much is happening in your world today. Remember to be beautiful – let your light shine from the inside out. It has nothing to do with outward appearances but rather the beauty of the love light you radiate out. The world is evolving and changing by letting this light shine and uplift others as well. Be beautiful today.'-StarChild 8-18-13

'Your personal truth is welling up. Who are you? What do you stand for? Are there things which you need to change, but have been reluctant to do so? These questions point one to the personal truth of one's soul essence. To be at the purest energy of one's soul, one must be truthful with oneself. Have you remembered that you are an unlimited being? That you are pure love? Beauty? Joy? Peace? You are all this and more. That is why when you are in sync with the ultimate vibration of love, manifestation comes easily and for the highest good. Remember you come form the stars, and that you carry the light to shine to those you encounter. This the vibration and carries the world to the next phase of ascension. Look for our signs in the sky as confirmation. You are ready and it is time.'-StarChild
8-15-13

'The time is now for contact and transformation. Be aware and mindful, as the current energetic shifts can cause chaotic activity that can lead to accidents, irritability and the like if not properly channeled. Remember to be in the vibration of love and to know that this is a most exciting time! Notice any densities leaving, and allow the light to take its place. All are transiting to a higher dimensional plane, so this is all good. Look to the north to east skies until the full moon comes. There is much activity and messages for you now. Be blessed, be kind, compassionate, and caring. Remember to care for others, including the being you live upon. Be light, love and peace, for that is where you are heading. We are well pleased, and are making our presence known. Be open and notice the subtle changes going on around you. It is time, and you are ready.'-StarChild
8-12-13

'Love is all around, though at times it may be hard for some to see. Reach out in kindness and compassion to those in need. All is love, and when that love is expressed towards another, all are blessed. We see you helping each other, and coming together in light and love. That is why you are now able to see us. We are here, helping you and guiding you, in congruence with your vibrations for love and peace. Peace is the goal, and that comes through love. Hold that vibration as you look to the northern sky tonight. Watch for the signs in the sky. Open your heart, be clear and vibrant, and be in sacred space as you come together in love and light. Honor the Earth and all her inhabitants, see the love and beauty in all things, and resonate in the love that drives the world into healing and restoration. We are pleased with your willingness and caring, and are here to help you and guide you. Watch for us tonight, we will be there.'-StarChild 8-8-13

'No matter what is happening – there is always hope. Hope fuel the change that changes the way things get done in this dimension. Soon you will understand how easily your thoughts manifest your reality, and will be able to get out of one's own way. Look deep into your spirit and see what your beliefs are. Do you have beliefs that limit you? Or do know that you are an unlimited being who is capable of doing whatever it is that you truly wish to do? You are unlimited, and can do whatever it is that you truly desire. Search inside and know that voice inside that drives your dreams is guiding you to the destination of your choice. Remember only love is real, and that which makes your heart sing drives you towards your path that you agreed to before you came here. Remember you are love and you are unlimited. Listen to what makes you happy and pursue that in love. That is your destiny.'-StarChild
8-5-13

'Notice the numbers that come into your field today. There are certain sequences of such numbers that carry vibrations to help one to connect to other dimensions. Notice if a certain number shows itself to you throughout the day, or throughout your life here. Each number carries a vibration to help you on your path. Numerical codes are contained within that open dimensional doorways to help to connect. Notice which numbers are appearing to you, as well as what the presence within those numbers reveals to you. You are being watched and guided daily, this is one way to notice our presence. Be mindful and aware, and gain insight in to which numbers are important for you.'-StarChild
8-1-13

'Storms may come and storms may go – but the steadfastness of faith remains. Once you realize that you are here to love and to serve, the way is made and the storm releases its grip, freeing one to pursue their purpose. The school that is the Earth dimension has many teachers, for you have planned it that way. You are now entering the time when your skills are to be put to the test. Know that when you vibrate in resonance to that which your heart knows, you are always on the right path. When you see the ships and feel our presence, you know you are being guided. We commune with you through many channels, through the sea, air and land, through the plant kingdom and through those you call animals. Each one is a guide in its own right, one that you have called upon to help you further your path. Listen with ears that hear and eyes that see, and know when your heart is pure, all good things truly come, as they are manifested from deep within your spirit. Honor all your teachers – in all their many forms – today.'–StarChild 7-27-13

'Kindness is the vibration of the day. Anything less is a cry for love, for love is all that is real. So love each other, be kind and strive for peace. Know that we are here, and we see your actions as well as your heart. Love can change anything, and we are happy to see you are doing just that. When you look to the sky tonight, and see the 'star' twinkle, know that we know that you know that we know, and we are very happy. Keep up the good work, and be kind to all.'-StarChild
7-24-13

'The beauty and love that one experiences everyday is the glue that holds the world as you know it together. This often happens through water or other crystalline structures, like crystals or even the fascia of living creatures. There is an intelligence and wisdom that is being shared at al times. The way to tap in to this huge library of knowledge is through love. It is also how to manifest one's life the way one wishes it to be. Joy, trust, love and happiness are integral to the manifestation process. As one observes the plants, and the love they radiate at all times, one can begin to 'tap into' different planes of consciousness. This was initiated on this planet, being, Earth, millennia ago as the great golden light poured from the ancestral ship into the great altar down to the essence of the core, and now lives in the life force of all, through the life force of the plants, and then the rest of life forms. This natural love and beauty is

abundant, and as all focus upon that, more abundance and beauty is created. Be mindful of what one focuses upon, for that is how the world will be to that being. See it through love, joy and beauty, and that vibration takes precedence, and is especially strong when multiple beings focus upon it together.'-StarChild
7-17-13

'There is wisdom hidden in the beings called plants. They have carried the information of the ascension discreetly for millennia. Some of you have tapped in to their special life force of love. Their vibration is one of love, light, power and healing – and the ability to bring visions to those who seek other dimensional realities. They keep the air breathable for humans, and the atmosphere intact. Without them, this planet would not be able to support life in the form of humans, as they circulate the breathe cycle with life forms. Honor their wisdom and beauty on this day, and notice how strong even the most 'fragile' among them are. Humans too have great strength, that when they tap in to the life force of the plant kingdom, they can find that strength in the love force of light. Some plants will speak to humans who seek enlightenment. It is time to have a conversation, or at least begin to listen to their vibration. The time of the now is the time to gain that wisdom that the plant kingdom holds. Honor them, and perhaps they will share some of their wisdom with you.'-StarChild 7-13-13

'Appreciate the rain, the wind, the day, the night. Each one perpetuates a cycle which afford you the opportunity to learn more about yourself and your mission here on Earth. What part of the cycle are you in? Are you calling life in, or releasing things which no longer serve you? Action or rest?All is building towards your fruition of this reality, your existence here, to love, learn and grow as you make your mark upon this planet, learn to cooperate in joy and love and be in the vibration of peace. Each cycle has a reason. Where are you in the cycle today?'-StarChild
7-10-13

'All is connected, be in peace. The waters, sky, and earth all have their life forms, all of which thrive in love. Together the love vibration increases the wellness of that which the attention is brought to. Bring your attention to those creatures who have no voice, and give them one through your own. Bring that love from your heart out to all the multiverse, for not only will be it returned multifold, but that is how you manifest that which is important to you. Be blessed, be in joy and love, and vibrate accordingly.'-StarChild
7-6-13

'Know that you are the pure light of innocence and grace. Have you forgotten that? It is time to honor those energies which you incarnated into this form with. Remember to play and to have fun, for that is the guidepost for where your path lies. At times, beings bring with them vibrations of trauma from the past and it deforms the present and prevents one from attaining their perfection. Honor the lessons learned and release any energy that hinders you from your pure light. You are light and love, and as you live your life from that place of truth, the light strings which make you who you are strengthen and glow. In health, harmony and peace, you reflect the true nature of your divine soul, so dance and play today.'-StarChild
6-28-13

'Your world is in transition. Love and prayers are needed to restore the balance of the planet you live upon. Restoration of the honeybees, birds, and other pollinators is crucial to the survival of this planet and of your species. All aspects are interconnected and interdependent. Send your love to both the microcosm and the macrocosm to bless this beautiful planet you live upon with your prayers and thought forms. Your love helps to restore this planet and vibrate this love harmoniously throughout the multiverse. It is time to honor those small beings whose presence is required for pollination and the bearing of fruit. Say thank you to the bees, butterflies, birds, bats, mammals and others who keep the natural world in balance. The world is changing, but with your love, this can be restored and the many species who depend upon this saved. The presence of loving beings together in unity sending vibrations of love and healing have great effect in the galactic world. This

translates to real world changes on this planet-being Earth. Send your love and your appreciation to all pollinators on this great day, for this is how the 'new' Earth is created. Love, light, joy and harmony are the building blocks to healing, it is now time to do this work.'-StarChild
7-1-13

'Be present. Mindfulness is the act of paying attention and giving your love to the situation at hand. What ever it is that you do today, do it with mindfulness, love, beauty and grace. Every act is a holy act. The very act of breathing is a holy act. Have you honored your breath today? It is what connects you to your spirit form. The reciprocal nature of the breathe reminds one of the connection between the body, mind and spirit. All are equally important, and as you breathe mindfulness into all your cells, the energetic exchange of vibration occurs. This often leads to feeling of calmness and well being. Bring that mindfulness into your awareness today, and breathe your blessings to all you encounter. Love is always returned, multiplied, when given freely from the heart. Bless your world, and be blessed in return. Mindfulness is the key.'-StarChild 7-3-13

'All is connected, be in peace. The waters, sky, and earth all have their life forms, all of which thrive in love. Together the love vibration increases the wellness of that which the attention is brought to. Bring your attention to those creatures who have no voice, and give them one through your own. Bring that love from your heart out to all the multiverse, for not only will be it returned multifold, but that is how you manifest that which is important to you. Be blessed, be in joy and love, and vibrate accordingly.'-StarChild 7-6-13

'Mindfulness is the key to the change you desire. Love allows the vibration to match that which is in one's heart, allowing the manifestation to occur more rapidly. Be of a grateful heart, and do your part as you watch your destiny unfold before you. Love, trust and knowingness go together. The new cycle is here, and the world as you know it is now more responsive to your thoughts. Make them for the good of all, and you will resonate with the heartbeat of this beautiful planet you live upon. Healing, joy and love is your vibration. Know it.'-StarChild 7-11-13

'We walk among you everyday. Some of you are awakening to know that you, too, come from the stars. Do not dismiss the synchronicities that are divinely inspired. You are being called to wake up and take your position. Many of you have already done that, and we are well pleased. You are stepping forth in light and love doing what you can to love the planet back into health. What you do has effects in the other galaxies as well as the one that Earth is in, for all is connected through the great web of light. Honor all the beings who have made the commitment to be part of the great awakening, including yourself. Help your fellow humans who are beginning to see things that previously they were blind to. The world as you know it has undergone some changes. It is in a new position to reveal the wonders of how magnificent and beautiful all creation can be. See clearly with eyes of love, and watch the reality reveal its' beauty. Love is what is true, and when one remains in that vibration of love, all

things are possible. Know that you, too, can change what you see, to make things vibrate with the divine love that you put out. Shine in the light, and know that you are part of the process at hand.'-StarChild
7-15-13

'Much illumination has been present of late. This is shown to you so you may know how to proceed with your gifts for the next phase of manifestation. Give thanks for these illuminations, for they are mirrors of you soul – showing you the potential of who you are. Honor these forms of your future self, for great things are being accomplished. Be in love, integrity, honesty and courage and watch your dreams become reality.'–StarChild
7-22-13

'So many blessings to be shared today. Each one of you has a gift to share to make this world vibrate in resonance to what it is you are calling in and manifesting. The ships are here, stationed throughout this blue globe. Some of you are seeing the beings that are operating these vessels as the time-space is bent around these objects. Although they may be cloaked, your love and intent allows one to see through with the pure heart of love, light and integrity. Greed, ego and misuse of power have no place in this new way. Love, cooperation, compassion and kindness pave the way for all to eventually see. The healing of this planet-being Earth, and the beings upon her is taking place, and now that this next cycle of light is now here, the manifestations are getting easier and appear quicker. You have done well in riding the wave of change, and in promoting that change. It comes from the joined hearts and minds that come together in purity, love and integrity to

make a better way. Share your blessings of love with each other today. You are making a beautiful difference.'-StarChild
7-25-13

'We are initiating contact with you today, are you able to hear us and connect? Look to the northern sky and ask for us to show you we are here. If you see what looks like a 'star' twinkle, then move, or blink, know that you are getting an answer. Some of you use channeling methods to hear our messages. Listen to what we tell you tonight. Many are receiving messages while they sleep and travel to other dimensions. Be in the vibration of love and belief, and be open to what is transmitted to you. Some of you hear us regularly, and know where to find us. Those that are now beginning, begin by being still and opening sacred space. There the vibration is pure and full of love. We communicate in the dimension of love, and when you feel the 'knowings' that come from inside, know that we are near. At times, an Earth being may appear and confirm what has just happened. This may be words said to you from another human, or a vibration transmitted from an animal or a plant. As you learn to trust your intuition, you will begin to 'hear' us more. Be in the vibration of pink as you look to the sky tonight. We are here, waiting to connect with you. In love, light and bliss for the good of all beings in all dimensions.'-StarChild 7-31-13

'Every day may have its challenges, but in those challenges lies the gifts. Once one figures that out, there are only blessings, as love is all that is truly real. Be the love you seek, and manifest the change that you sense is here, for it is, and you are creating it with each intentional thought you think. Great blessings are here and more are coming – do not be sidetracked with the blasts that distract. Know who you are and where you come from. We are here to remind you that you originate from the stars, and that this blip in time, though short lived, is a learning experience in how to make the multiverse a better place for all. It all begins with kindness and love. We are watching and connecting. Notice the synchronicities and know that we are here.'-StarChild
8-2-13

'Keep going and stay strong. The world as you create it comes to fruition by staying the course. Remember you have all the power that you need, yet often you do not remember your own power. Remember that you are an unlimited being and that fear has no place in your life. Courage, kindness, peace and love are your natural birthrights – that is what you came into this world with. Remember you are on this Earth for only a short time. You are here to learn your life lessons, bring your essence to the world for the greater good, while bringing joy to your soul in doing so. Bless the world with your light, be strong and stay your course. You are closer than you think.'-StarChild 8-6-13

'Extraneous issues are flying off to reveal the essence of who you really are. You are being honed, purified and transformed into the highest of your being. Let go of that which no longer serves, so that you may grasp the next level of awakening which is now occurring. Some are noticing phenomena of dimensional activity not previously encountered. This new level of vibration is what you are being acclimated to. Soon it will be normal for you, and as your gifts continue to develop, more and more will be revealed to honor the essence of love, and pour it forth. Prepare to stretch your mind today as situations flip unexpectedly. Remember it is all in divine right order, and all is leading towards peace. It is time, and you are ready.'-StarChild
8-13-13

'Your personal truth is welling up. Who are you? What do you stand for? Are there things which you need to change, but have been reluctant to do so? These questions point one to the personal truth of one's soul essence. To be at the purest energy of one's soul, one must be truthful with oneself. Have you remembered that you are an unlimited being? That you are pure love? Beauty? Joy? Peace? You are all this and more. That is why when you are in sync with the ultimate vibration of love, manifestation comes easily and for the highest good. Remember you come form the stars, and that you carry the light to shine to those you encounter. This the vibration and carries the world to the next phase of ascension. Look for our signs in the sky as confirmation. You are ready and it is time.'-StarChild
8-15-13

'Much is happening in your world today. Remember to be beautiful – let your light shine from the inside out. It has nothing to do with outward appearances but rather the beauty of the love light you radiate out. The world is evolving and changing by letting this light shine and uplift others as well. Be beautiful today.'-StarChild 8-18-13

'Enjoy this day of opportunities and happiness. Today your projects that you have been channeling receive a boost from the cosmos. It is time to put yourself out there and reap the benefits of what your gift is – as you share it with others. Honor your gifts, share them, and in kindness, compassion and love restore the light to yourself and this planet you live upon. Beam the love to others as you shine upon this earth. Remember you are love and light – so show that to others today.'-StarChild 6-20-13

'You have answered the call for love and are proceeding with the divine mission for which you are here. Love, kindness, and compassion assist the goal of peace. The Divine light is seen by all, and those who understand their mission are guided by that light, which dwells within. Illuminate yourself, know that you are guided and loved, and that which you truly desire is on it's way if not already manifested. Look to the signs in the skies, for we are appearing in more places to show you the way. Unconditional love paves the way for non-judgement and universal peace. Seek that in yourself and watch as your reality reflects that mindset. The world one inhabits bends via vibrations of thought, therefore be mindful, loving and kind. You are loved, and are love. Show it.'-StarChild
6-23-13

'The energies are strong – and some of you are learning about yourselves in alternate realities. Realize you are more than you think, and your talents and interests reflect that. Shine on from the bright light within you and discover your own secrets of eternity hiding within you. This shell you possess, your human suit – is but one of many suits you wear. The next two weeks will show you more about who you truly are. Be ready, watch the skies and vibrate with divine love. You are ready for the next ascension phase.'-StarChild
6-9-13

'The new ways are now. Each thought that you think that is positive and directive is a step towards your future self. The doors to abundance are opening, but it is up to you to walk through and take your place. Have no fear, walk in courage into your own future that you are creating right now. With love, kindness and compassion, know that the seeds you sow today will reap rewards. Where and how you plant is up to you. We are here to guide you; look inside and listen to that small still voice of your personal inner truth. Vibrate to that call of love, and watch your star family show you the way. Remember you are love, and are called to share that love in whatever way is appropriate to your vibration. Enjoy this time, and beam that vibration of wholeness and love to all in kindness and compassion.'-StarChild
6-15-13

'Truths are revealed and challenges overcome. It is a time of ushering in new ways of being that resonate with your eternal essence. Speak your truth and be aligned with the vibration of peace, love and joy that comes from within. This may mean examining your point of view on some issues to determine your true feelings, rather than merely accepting what you have been told is the truth. Your inner senses are showing you the way for your personal and collective being. Be thankful for all of these experiences for they have helped to shape you in to who you have now become. Listen to your still inner voice for that is where the truth is. Be full of courage as you speak your truth, for in doing so, you are liberated from misperceptions. You know where you are going and what you need to do, it is written on your soul. Tune in and listen, we are here to help you. Go in joy, peace, and kindness as you change the world from within. In beauty, love and truth.'-StarChild
6-7-13

'The ships are activated to the corners of the Earth to offer help and hope to those in need. Be of good cheer and send your loving vibrations to help to come together and shift the outcome of the situations at hand. Love is all that is real and as such, the love sent through the ether combines together to strengthen the frequency and manifest in the consensual reality. Keep in the vibration of love and light and listen to your star family who is there guiding you at each step. You are light and love and as you radiate that out to the world you live in, it creates a flow of goodness that transforms at the energetic level first, then the physical level. Stay strong and clear and do not be distracted by what the others who live in fear may say. Know the love will always prevail and that you are responsible for your part of the love. Stay strong and focused and know that each quantum of love that you send out to the multiverse is matched by that of

the star family for the greatest good. Earth is important to the entire galaxy, and as you love your world back to her wholeness, you are strengthened and healed along with the Earth. Be strong and full of love and know that all that you do is noted. Remember YOU create your own reality. Make it matter.'-StarChild
6-4-13

'Today is a good day to smile and be thankful for all that has been manifested. We are watching and are well pleased. You are realizing that love is the only answer, and that love is what you are made of. Be happy and full of joy. We will begin to visit again in the next few days, till then rest and enjoy your creations.'-StarChild 6-2-13

'Portals are opening up throughout this Earth world. Surrender to the light and allow for the manifestations of your highest self to come to fruition. The time is now to make things happen, for the energy is one of clarity, focus and vision. Surrender to your purpose of light and love – and prepare for great things.'-StarChild
5-30-13

'Look for the ways in which spirit has answered your call for manifestation. It might not be in the way in which you think. Once you realize that you create everything, it is easier to manifest that which you desire more quickly. Your thoughts create your world, so make your thoughts peaceful, kind and full of joy. You just may realize that you are co-creating the new world in which light and love of the conscious rules, and all are treated equally important. As you love your fellow beings, the love is returned, and that which is manifested is of the purest vibration. That pure vibration has the power to heal all. What you think matters – so think and be – love.'-StarChild 5-29-13

'Ships of pink and yellow will grace your sky tonight Be present for these ships bring messages from the star families of the Pleiades and from andromeda Face west and north to receive your message and be blessed with the divine ray of the light of the one known as Michael. His sword of truth will illuminate that which is for you to pursue for your souls mission. Be mindful and flow.'-StarChild 5-23-13

'The contact continues. The emphasis today is over the polar regions. The main mother ship is in place over the 'northern' pole, while another, equally impressive ship hovers over the 'southern' pole. In doing this, both poles are being vibrated with the energy of love to protect the glaciers, the source of the currents of water, air and therefore life. This will be their docking station for the immediate time, while the satellite ships are very busy making contact with those who are in positions of leadership, especially in those regions which are very fragile at this moment in time. The message to day is one of cooperation, love and hope. As all beings, those on this planet, and those off planet vibrate together with the plan of peace, it shall be done. Ships are stationed outside the militarily sensitive areas in the middle East, but it is the vibration of love that will shift the energy and bring a true and lasting peace. There is no plan to interfere, but will do so if it becomes absolutely necessary. Send your love to all beings, and vibrate today from a heart of compassion and kindness. There is uncertainty in the air, by focusing on the love and the peace – which is coming – one helps to bring in this reality sooner.'-StarChild 5-13-13

'The mothership is stationed here right now. Ships are present all over this Earth, and all star nations are represented. Open your heart and mind, and connect from your light center. We are here. The paradigm is shifting, and your world is expanding. Smile, this is the new beginning and many of you already sense this and have made contact. Some of you have had contact but are just not aware of it, as it may come in the form of a dream or a symbol one sees frequently. That is your family showing you they are around, guiding you to find them. What a joyous day for humankind!'-StarChild 5-10-13

'Can you hear our call to you? We show up in your dreams, and for some will show up in your waking reality. Some of you are being invited upon ships for the very first time. Others, who are familiar with this process already, are now bringing others aboard. This is to acquaint humans with the new paradigm of multi galactic world beings coming together to serve the light. This means thought patterns of destructive actions must stop, and respect and honor of the natural world must once again be brought to the forefront of the way of the law of love. It has always been the way, and is what every indigenous culture learned from their starfamily so very long ago. Honor, love and respect go hand in hand, and as such, give love and healing in return. Those who seek to harm the Earth will be held responsible for their vibrations, as all beings are everywhere. The vibrations of honor, love and respect will heal the wounds which have been allowed to be inflicted. The lessons are

almost over. What have you learned? Be true to your inner light and you will never go astray, for that is your true self, the way that we see you. You are light and love, and can shift your world instantly. You do not yet realize what power you hold in creating the new way of being.
5-9-13

'Stay pure and focused no matter what is going on around you today. Radiate love and stay in the vibration of peace, tranquility and harmony. Many distractions abound today, so keep focused and you will not deviate from your path. Listen to the voice inside that hears our call. You know what to do and how to do it. Be of strength and courage, focused and pure, and you will continue to ascend. Be one with the natural world, and look to the skies once again tonight. Be open and connect. We will see you there.'-StarChild
5-6-13

'Although you long for the tranquility of your star family, one may bring that tranquility and peace to Earth through vibrational resonance. By bringing the star ways here on Earth, with intention, the communication portal, a vortex of sorts may be established. Choose a place where you go to on a near daily basis. An altar in your home is a good start. By meditating and bringing in the resonance of the star family, you bring it to fruition. As the energetic quanta of your holiness permeates that designated space, the vibrational quality of that space transforms to a holy place of contact. We are everywhere, awaiting an invitation of contact by you. By meditating in the sacred place and calling us in, we will come. We are always here, but by being in that sacred space, one is more likely to sense out presence, hear our messages, and even see our forms. We love you, and look forward to meeting with you once more.'-StarChild 5-5-13

'Today there is a smoother transition to the higher plane. Prepare to meet with your star family. We have heard your calls for disclosure and are very near. Some of you will see us tonight, others will feel our presence. Take the time to be in the natural environment and to honor the local places near you. We often connect to humans through the presence of the temples located in the natural realms. Although often obscured by dimensionality, these places are being revealed as the vibration of the quantum number of humans is approaching critical mass, making it more easily accessed by those on Earth. Those with the eyes to see and the ears to hear are finding the guidance which has been here all along much easier to know now. It is a good day to plan the direction you seek, and be open to guidance as to how to go about it. Look for us tonight in the northeast sky, and meditate on the colors pink and gold. Open your heart and connect. We love you and are here for you. Be in kindness, love and peace, and connect to us tonight.'-StarChild 5-4-13

'Sudden shifts of energy are on target for today. Some of you may feel these shifts, or feel more intensely the fields that surround you. This clearing and shifting is to allow peace to come through you, with humility, kindness and compassion. That which is important to you is being brought up and you must decide what you are to do about it. It is time. Clarity is the theme of the day, although it may come after an intense energetic impact. Be mindful of these shifts and ride the waves consciously as to not get caught off guard, especially in the emotional realm. Remember you have created these situations to make the multiverse a better place and to ascend to a higher plane. Remember you are perfect love, and reflect that to the world today.'-StarChild
5-3-13

'You are called to manifest light. It matters not where you are, nor who you are with, nor what situation you may be in, let the light shine through you. Be light, love, harmony, peace, kindness and compassion you wish to see in your world. Be firm in your convictions of peace, and choose not to engage in energies that are not in alignment. You are light and love. Resonate that today.'-StarChild 5-2-13

'Another day of integration unfolds. Mysteries are being revealed and those with the eyes to see and the ears to hear are understanding the messages being written in one's heart. What makes you happy is being revealed, as is whether the structure of your current way of life is compatible with that. Many of you have taken steps to be in congruence with the vibrations of love and peace. This will provide a sense of well being and provide a foundation for you to do your soul work through. If this is not yet the case with you, it is time to look at the steps you need to take to make that happen in your life . You came here with a plan, are you fulfilling that? Yes, you are exactly where you are 'supposed' to be. Look and acknowledge the path you have taken to get where you are. Say thank you to all circumstances, for they have make you who you are – just as you had planned long before you incarnated into this human form to learn duality. You are now learning that only love is real, and that love comes from within. There are multiple ways of expressing that love. Which way are you expressing it today?'-StarChild 4-30-13

'Today is a bit more serene. Accept the gifts, and listen to the dreams that have been given. It is time to integrate the lessons learned over the past few few days and to begin to put the pieces together. The intensity will return, but this quiet period is to have you prepare in love and peace for the next phase. The cycle shifts from light to dark to light again, all with the energies of release, transformation and growth. It is now time for growth. Be clear on what it is you wish to grow, for what you manifest is in direct relationship to what vibrations you put out. Be therefore in love, and all good things shall come eventually Honor your past and where you have been to call in an even brighter future. Remember you are a holy being and as a spirit of light are called to bring goodness wherever you go. Enjoy today.'-StarChild
4-26-13

'The clearings continue today, but also the lessons and gifts are being revealed now. You are stronger than you think, and what you manifest is a product of your vibrations. Healing, love, kindness and compassion are growing the new world of this multiverse. Be kind to yourself, be kind to others, and be kind to the world(s). Kindness is a form of love, and the one that is the dominant one for today. Spread the love and allow the gifts of the past few days to integrate in to your field. Continue the vibration of love, for that is all that is real, and is what shapes the time construct which is called the future.'-StarChild
4-23-13

'Stand firm – the next few days will continue to see the energy amplify, with intense clearings, releases and downloads. Many are receiving gifts, some of which may not appear as such at the time, but they are. You are becoming stronger and more defined, honing in on what it is you seek to create with your intentions. Your thoughts carry great power, and is why is so important that they contain love and kindness. You are the shining light. Remember only love is real, and is shown by the light. Be strong, be kind, and be of one mind, for the codes of Lemuria are continuing to imprint upon this planet being and restore her as well as all living beings in this dimension. Continue the love, it is all that is real.'-StarChild
4-22-13

'Light is shining through even the tiniest of cracks. When things seems dark, remember there is always a filament of light and bring that forward to cleanse and clarify the space. Channel the light in whatever you do and bring peace through with that light. We are in the skies tonight, watch for us as we send you signals of love on your path. Breathe in the love, and listen for our presence. We are here, and the time for disclosure draws near. When the amount of people on this planet reaches the quantum number to accept our presence, we will be shown publicly. That time draws near. Those who claim leadership on this planet know of our presence. You know of our presence. Soon all will know and will see that we have been here all along, shining that light into the tiniest of cracks. You are the light. Shine everywhere and bless your worlds.'-StarChild
4-21-13

'Kindness is the vibration of the day. Many of the humans are hurting. Love heals all and is all that is truly real, all else is an illusion. Please be kind to all creatures of every species and environments – the land, sea, sky, space, inter-dimensional, and to yourself as well. Let that love permeate through out the multi-verse, and deliver it with kindness.'-StarChild 4-16-13

'The ancient codes of Lumeria have been released and the transformation has begun. Shifts are occurring, and the golden age is once again upon this planet. This planet has reached the quanta of souls necessary to shift it to the next dimensional phase. Continue to remember to honor and respect the land, your ancestors, the waters, stars and seas. All beings are sacred and as such deserve the love and respect that lives in one's hearts. Magnify that love and the dimensional aspects of the codes now implanted will spring into fruition sooner. It is a most blessed time to be upon this planet being, Earth. Glorify this day and all of its potential. You are reaping your rewards of the prayers you have prayed, the love you have shared and the kindness you show. Be amazing!'-StarChild 4-8-13

'Your culture is calling you to spend the time in sacred space as you were taught. Even if you feel you have no 'culture,' remember all traditional practices come from the stars. Your ancestors came here long ago to teach the ways of the stars to the humans. You hare now here in human form to remember that. As you honor the way of the light, and realize that all life is connected you are connecting to the ancient 'culture' of the stars. You may honor your star culture by practicing tolerance, peace, reverence and respect for nature, love, kindness and compassion. This is but a start. To bring in the new Earth ways, one must learn to recognize one's self in the 'other' who or what ever that may be – a rock, a tree, a turtle, a mountain, the sea, a child, an elder, a man or a woman. Embody each one for they are you and you are they. Each traditional culture on Earth is based on light. Embody that and be as one. It is time to integrate the star culture of light on

Earth and get back to the 'roots' of your society. We are here to help you with that process.'-StarChild 4-4-13

'Higher orders of being are the mode of this day. This may take the form of releasing unneeded energy or incorporating new energy to achieve balance and growth. Some situations may have a tendency to 'pop' to allow for the field to grow. All is shifting towards a higher order. sometimes to do that it is necessary to stratify your field to determine what stays and what goes. The choice is up to you, and how you choose to proceed form here will determine the rate and direction in which you grow. Movement and change coincide with the cycles of the sun, moon and stars as perceived from this planet being Earth. As a human incarnate, one is tuned to this cycle from the Earth's perspective. Acknowledge this and flow with the tides of change. We are here to help you and guide you as you anchor in the light frequencies that have been given to humanity via the light codes. This process of awakening is creating the golden age, but steps must still be taken by those who carry the codes to

allow this process to happen. You are called to create a kinder, more compassionate Earth. You carry the codes. It is now time to use them and evolve.'–StarChild
3-28-13

'The time cycle of the monthly moon is given to reflect aspects of your spirit. The being of the moon, together with the being of the Earth, combine to create the forces which are compatible with human life. Honor the cycle of the light and of the moon, and realize your tissues follow that cycle as well. Some may have insights from their Star family, or be awakened by the intensity of the light of the moon, illuminating deep aspects, often hidden during other times of the month. Each moon is a gift that illuminates aspects of one's soul. Treat each day like the gift it is, one more day in human form on Earth. This time does not last long before you return to pure Spirit, so enjoy.'-StarChild
3-27-13

'Today is a good day to make your dreams come true. Take the initiative to make progress in that which you have come here to do. The time for excuses is over, for you know that you create your own reality. We are here, and guide you on your path, for your essence is very clear about what it is you are here to be. You are love, kindness, compassion and truth. Your being-ness is the outgrowth of your love. Only love is real, and your way of expressing that love to the world is what makes you the happiest. That which lights up your heart is the path to follow, for the goodness contained in that spark of light is your roadmap. We are here to guide, but you are the one who must go and fulfill your destiny. You create everything. What are you creating today?'-StarChild 3-22-13

'Being in tune with the natural world allows one to 'see' with other senses than those typically thought of. Some can learn to feel colors, or know the sound of a leaf, while others can understand the history in the rock they hold. Listen to this planet being yo live upon and realize that you are intimately connected, the way your liver, kidney and heart are connected to your brain. All flows together for the understanding of the highest good of all. Listen to your natural world and know that the answers are there. Learning to decipher what is being said, and you will begin to navigate from a ever increasing vibrant point of view for your good and the good of those who inhabit this multiverse with you.'-StarChild
3-20-13

'Today is a reminder to be happy. We are in the oceans, connecting to the grid that animates this planet being, Earth. Honor your natural world, and know that the presence of love that connects all to all, resides in you too. The energetic flow of life is present within you. Be in motion, get rid of that which no longer serves, and embrace that which makes you happy.
Happiness is a road map. Enjoy your journey.'-StarChild
3-19-13

'We operate out of deep underwater bases that are connected to the stars. Some of you have seen lights come out of deep waters, showing you the presence that resides there. The intermediaries that we work through, the whales, dolphins, seals, turtles, rays, corals, fish and more sea family, show the way to balance the being that is the sea. These beings protect and guide the forces that make up the currents, and weather. This ecosystem drives the engine of the entire being Planet Earth, and must be kept pure and clean. Each being plays an important part of the entire ecosystem, and the functioning of this planet. All is connected, and through the undersea bases there is a network that connects the grid that produces the telluric currents which help us to navigate this planet. Star family will always find you when you are ready and open. Occasionally one will be revealed to open a person and wake them up to their real existence as a star child. Do

you realize that you are from the stars and that all is connected through the waters? Give thanks to the waters today, those in the seas, lakes, rivers, clouds, rains, snow, and those in your own bodies. Resonate with the power of love and transform the vibrations throughout the multiverse as you do. It is time.'-StarChild
3-18-13

'Storm clouds come to clear the air and water the sprouts of new beginnings. New codes are coming and those who are prepared will be able to feel the shift today. Activation is continuing and as you pass through this next phase, you will be pointed in the next direction. Star family will be present in the skies tonight. Look for ships, lights or orbs, and know we are there. You are beginning to see us, and to acknowledge the energetic presence that surrounds all beings on this planet. This presence surrounds you as well, and is how we connect to you and all living beings simultaneously. Listen to the wisdom in the trees, rocks, animals and plants and you will know the wisdom that resides in you as well. All is connected through love.'-StarChild
3-16-13

'Clarity is the order of the day. Experiences have been showing contrast to show what to keep and what to discard. Clarify your intent and bring in the joy. You are a child of the light, and your Star family is watching over you, guiding you to create the life you have chosen for yourself before you incarnated to Earth. Do you feel the flow of energy resonating with the way you conduct your life? Are you in tune with your environment, and with the stars? Can you sense the wisdom in the animals and plants? the rocks? the formations left here long ago? They all contain wisdom to point the way to your own awakening, which is unfolding now. The light has been downloaded into your DNA. Be joyful and spread that joy to others, for in doing so you co create the field of joy that heals, regenerates, and renews. All is well.'-StarChild
3-13-13

'Call in the energy of how you wish to create your life. Do you yet realize that you create everything and that all is love? You have already planned this on some level before you came in to being in this form on this living being, the one called Earth, Gaia, Pachamama, and many other names. Names are a vibration and you can choose how to call yourself. It is time to realize your true nature and the ability that you have to call in your life the way you choose. When you choose love and the highest Divine will for all, your choices become clearer. Remember too, that you are an unlimited spiritual being who is having a human experience. You chose to be here, and you came with a mission connected to love. It is time to realize how you are to fulfill this mission.'-StarChild
3-12-13

'Vibrations continue to push towards a highest order. Decisions need to be made. In some instances, people, ideas or things will need to be let go. In some other instances, new ways of being must be adapted. Listen to the the calling of the divine in your heart – you will then know the way on which to proceed. The higher order is coming, and you have all been prepared. Today is decision time. What is your intention on how to live your life from today forward? Prepare and decide today.'-StarChild
3-11-13

'Vibrations are aligning to take things to a higher order. This can take the form of things breaking and needing repair, or insights that come like a flash out of 'nowhere.' Ride the waves and see where the energy leads. All are being directed to the next phase of ascension and awareness. Keep your ears and eyes open and discover your next quantum leap. This is necessary to bring you closer to your pure energetic state, and to separate truth from want. Listen with your heart, and know that all is okay, for truly the path before you may take several directions – each one is up to you. Listen to decipher the path for you now. It might be different than one you might of chosen before. You are evolving and growing, your luminous threads of DNA are beginning to integrate those attributes of which you were downloaded during these previous times. More growth is at hand. Be joyful as you become more light incarnate, the light human, homo-luminous. Activate your life and watch your changes as you continue this evolution of your spirit.'-StarChild 3-8-13

'The intense energies of the past few days give a break today. It is time to integrate the lessons learned from the sharp twists and turns of late, and leap into a higher quantum state. Practicality and spirituality go hand in hand, and kindness is key. Honesty, trust and communication are what is needed to resolve any lingering rifts. Put the ego aside and communicate from your heart. Humanity is entering a higher state of awareness, but still has a way to go. You can make that happen in your world with kindness, love, trust and appreciation. Your needs will always be met. As you trust, your Star family responds and makes the way known. Be in courage and in faith, and boldly go make your world a better place.'-StarChild
3-5-13

'Love trust and appreciation – these are the vibrational qualities your Star family asks humans to adhere to. When one is out of balance, one typically is deficient in one of these three attributes. Check to see if you are living in the love, trusting the Divine that all will work out for the highest good and appreciating all that is in your field. For if you are, your vibration on Earth will be one of peace – and that peace will spread, for that is the true nature of light humans.'-StarChild
3-1-13

'Remember that all form is light incarnate. That includes humans. As such, it is important that which you ingest, either by mouth, ears or eyes, should be of the most high. Bathe in the vibrations of love, truth and kindness, and that is what you will bring to others. Little green plants offer their love to you in the form of food for your physical bodies. They concentrate the light into nutrition for you. Honor them as they bring light in to your bodies, and increase your ability to decipher the vibrations in which we communicate to you. Liquid sunshine grows on your trees, and in your green foods. Take the time to honor those beings who have made it their job to provide you with ultimate nutrition to fuel your path with love. They are kin to the giant trees and to the tiniest plankton. Many are very old souls, and have come to hold space and to teach those who have the ears to hear and the eyes to see. Listen, and vibrate accordingly. They have a lot to teach you.'-StarChild

2-27-13

'Gifts abound from the inter-dimensional realms today. Those whom you call angels are having a celebration today, so look to find them everywhere. When you see a special sparkle in the eyes and feel that feeling in your heart, know that you are in the presence of someone special. Acknowledge that being with your holiness, and know that is the way of love. Honor, kindness and respect are the vibrations of the celebration today. Do so to all you encounter, and see if you cannot catch a glimpse of those beings around you today.'-StarChild 2-26-13

'Today is the day of appreciation. Thank the ones who originally brought the gift of life to your planet, and permeated it with the spirit of love. Remember that you, too, bring the life and love to this great galactic being called Earth, and as you love her, she in turn provides all that you could ever need. This mutual love churns the energy and keeps it flowing to provide the energetic continuum of this world. Each time you think a loving thought or do a kind deed, you add to this continuum of light, helping to keep all in balance on this lovely being of Earth. Remember to thank and honor her in the way you live your life. You are only in human form for a short while, make the time here count.'-StarChild
2-24-13

'Can you hear your Star family calling you? The energies are very high today. Listen and connect. Messages are coming through – not only for you, but your family and your worlds as well. Walk sacred today – and every day – and take the time to appreciate your natural world. Connect to the mountain and to the sea, for we are in both places and have made ourselves visible to you today. Bring flowers, cleanse with sage and salt, and be with holy water and oils. Prepare yourself for the attunement you are to receive today. Be aware and listen. Today is a most auspicious day.'–StarChild
2-21-13

'Remember that your prayers heal. Intention and focus brings the energy into a lazer-like precision to bring about the intended results with love, forgiveness and thanksgiving. When many are focused simultaneously on a energetic stream together, this focused energetic charge can move millions of beings together, through the power of oneness and cohesiveness. When done from the place of unconditional love, room is left for the miracles to occur, without any anticipation of a specific result. Often what occurs is much greater than any expectation. Expectations can hinder the progress, for often one thinks too 'small.' Know that greatness lies in all of you, and together with focused beams of love you truly are changing your world with love, peace and kindness. We are watching, and are very proud of you.'-StarChild
2-20-13

'Let the love flow out and touch all that you encounter today. Remember that you are a holy being, and as such all that you do, say and think are holy as well. How can you make your world a better place? It matters not where you live or what you do, but rather who you are. Be of one heart, one mind and bring the vibration of love to all, for that is who you truly are.'-StarChild 2-19-13

'Send love to all throughout your world today. Be kind and do real good where ever you are in what ever capacity you are able to. Today will challenge you, remain centered and feel the chord of light that anchors you to all other chords of light – uniting in a symphony. Vibrate together in love, be kind and know all is well.'-StarChild 2-15-13

'Love in action is required today. Your living planet is in need of assistance by those of you who live upon her. She gives you everything you have ever needed, and the reciprocal nature of energy flow dictates that the love you show feeds back into the energy pulse that generates the very essence of life throughout the multiverse. Many of you have taken from her without reciprocating the flow of love and light back to her. Simple acts, such as truly being thankful and tapping in to the energy that permeates all living beings – including this planet you live upon – generate an energy flow that keeps the systems in balance. This is important for the humans. The great galactic being called Earth has more than enough love and has given that unconditionally for eons. The humans, however, must realize that they, too, must vibrate the love for this planet. Love in action may be as simple as a prayer of thanks, or as complicated as designing and implementing a way to

clean up the oceans and the air from the toxicity of human life upon her. However you decide to honor, love and protect her, that will vibrate back in to your being-ness. Be as one, love fully and take the action to show your love. Pray, chant, sing, tone, do your ceremonies and sing your songs. Honor those who have gone before you and have shown you these ways. Your mother, Earth, is listening, and awaiting your response.'-StarChild
2-14-13

'The StarFamily that lives under the sea is reminding you that they, too, come from the stars. They have set up bases here on this planet, Earth, deep under the oceans to have a place to return to, and to operate from. Some of you have seen the bright lights and seen the deep depths from which the work is done. The ocean family has connections in space, and the beings who live in the sea, hold this world together with their vibrations of love. The dolphins, whales, rays, and other creatures patrol the oceans and keep the balance. Some of the others who live there are more humanoid in nature, and few have seen them. Remember them as you, too, seek balance in your own life. On this new day, go forth and cherish those relationships that make this world flow. You are one with this world, go forth and be the love that makes this flow. Remember that love fuels the world and heals all things, for that is all that is truly real. Human are mostly water. Go and bless your water star family today, and thank them for what they do. Then ask yourself how you can make a difference in the well being of the oceans, streams, and other forms of water. Listen for the answers, and go with the flow.'-StarChild 2-10-13

'The star family that lives under your seas is requiring your attention. As beings who live upon this great being called Earth, one must be aware of the great importance of the seas. The ocean family that lives here has bathed the Earth with the vibrations of wholeness from the beginning. They now require your help to sustain their task. Do what you can today to shift the direction of the health of the seas. Vibrate with the consciousness of the ocean family and restore the vibration of vitality and well being. They are a part of you as you are a part of them. Be one and unite in love, kindness and compassion. Give them your vibration of love, and seek ways to do tangible good on your Earth. This is your task today and always, as when you take care of your brothers and sisters in the sea (or air, or Earth, or sky) you are also taking care of yourself and those you love. All are connected, and all must be together in harmony for the restoration to occur. Do your part today, and know that we are here with you, helping you every step of the way.'-StarChild 2-7-13

'As you go about your day doing that which you came here to do, remember that everything you do, say and think is holy. You are a child of the stars, and as such, the light lives in you and in all that you do. Be mindful of your actions, for they speak more loudly than your words, and effect all in your field. Your kindness, compassion and love also affects all in your field, and helps to bring about the resonance of well being to all beings everywhere in the multiverse. Realize that all beings are connected, and what effects one affects another. Therefore be kind and full of compassion, for you are growing the new world. The legacy of peace you leave here on this being, Earth, sustains the future for the next seven generations. Be mindful of that and act accordingly.'-StarChild
2-5-13

'Today is a day to go forth with those vibrations of knowingness. You have been thinking and planning of how to go about what it is you wish to do. Listen to the small, still voice inside that is directing you. Which choice seems brightest – or seems to glow? Your star family is guiding you forward bringing that into fruition. Be ready to step into that which you create. You are ready. Honor the path which you have taken to get here and move forth in dignity and elegance – and always in integrity.'-StarChild
2-4-13

'Enjoy this day of relative quiet and peace. The cycle is swinging as the equilibrium is being re-established. Notice how many layers you have shifted through, and realize that your essence is becoming more and more congruent and focused – more authentically you. You know what is important to you, and as you look to the sky you wait for us to show ourselves to you. Some of you have seen us, some of you have heard us, and some of you have intuited us. We know your challenges and are here to help. Look inward to your truest essence to find the source where the communication is at its finest. Be still and look within to the internal sun that lights your spirit. There, the dimensions intersect to show you the way to your own divine truth. Honor that truth and walk it each day. Your strength of spirit is gaining each day. Allow and enjoy and be in peace.'-StarChild
2-1-13

'A new order begins. Many of you are working with us to bring about the change that is happening. We see you and want you to know we support your actions, as they are filled with good intentions and right purpose. We remind you to always check your motives to make sure they come from the purest place of integrity and honor. By remaining in the highest vibration of love and light the path of integrity is maintained.'-StarChild
1-30-13

'Today is a reminder to ground. Although you may long for your home in the stars, there is still work to be done here, so bring the stars down to the earth and be as one. Connect with this beautiful planet that you live upon, for she, too, is from the heavens upon which you gaze. Remember she provides all your needs for this incarnation. Thank her for that. Realize that you, too, are a part of the sea, stars, Earth, birds, fish, mammals, insects, plants and more which live in a balanced harmony in this ecosystem. Realize your place in your world, and act accordingly. Love this being, and realize that the love you give will be returned in multitude! Love is all that is real, and as such, also the only thing that grows the more you give away. Send that vibration of love in to all that you do. Feed every spirit you encounter with love, including your own. As you

take care of each other, you are also taken care of, for all your needs will always be met. Trust, love and appreciation are keys, ground those vibrations into your being. You are love, you are light – show it to your world.'-StarChild
1-26-13

'Retreat in to the flow of nature – there you can hear your own voice come from within to guide you on this day. The natural world will always speak if you are still enough to listen. Whether your vibration needs uplifting or calming, nature always provides the way to balance. You also hold this within your own self. Breathe your breathe into any part of you that feels tense and release with the outgoing breath. Repeat until you feel calm. Nature flows as an example of how to live as a human. Be one with the trees, stars, and seas, and know that you, too, are love. Your beauty provides a balance in the universe that you may not even be aware of. Know that you are loved and watched over, and sent guiding messages daily. Look for us everywhere, for you will find us when you look. We love you and are so very happy you are you. Smile and be happy. Your star family is watching you!-StarChild
1-25-13

'Stand firm for what is important to you. Respect, honor and love are key to be in the flow of what matters. See the joy that emanates from your soul as you are true to your purpose and vibration. Love is the only vibration, but is manifest in many forms. Do not with hold this love, but embrace it, and watch your life transform. You are here to transform this world and bless it with your presence. Keep being the vibration that is you. It is beautiful.'-StarChild
1-24-13

'Respect and honor each other as there is truly only one. The being you live on is as much you as the birds, fish, and mammals that you share her with. Live your life with the consciousness of peace, love, harmony and kindness, and together your worlds will be restored. You have gone through the trials and tribulations which have forced you to examine what is important to you. It is now time to honor yourself, by honoring all, to bring this respect to all everywhere. You are creating the new Earth with each thought you think, each word you speak, and each action you take. It is time to coordinate those into a plan which is for the benefit of all. You know what you must do, it is now time to do it.'-StarChild
1-22-13

'Today is an opportunity to decipher how to proceed down your path. You have choices before you......which one seems to glow with possibilities? which makes your heart happy? you know what you are to do, thank the universe for the lessons learned and the opportunities that lay ahead. We can see the outcome, and although you may struggle at times with which one is the correct path for you, deep inside you know which route you will eventually take. Be joyful and know that all is good.'-StarChild
1-21-13

'Ride the roller coaster of up and downs today with grace and ease. Enjoy the bumps as they show you the depth that you can stretch and still not break – once you realize that you can never 'break' – only grow more flexible – you can enjoy the process for what it is – a wild ride in the circus you call life. Then it becomes an adventure to see how much fun you can have. Enjoy today.'-StarChild
1-17-13

'Today is a great day of hope and opportunity. The fabric of the multiverse has been opened to allow the spontaneous flow of the consciousness of light to show through. Expect more miracles and a general feeling of helpfulness among those you encounter. Realize this paves the way for all to enter with love, for those of this realm as well as the others in the multiverse. Parties are taking place celebrating today. Dance and be grateful for this time has come. It has not always been easy, but the rewards are great. It is now the time of the great quantum leap for humanity. Embrace this in love and light and be your peace. This spontaneously affects all, so smile and show others your love, and let this love shine everywhere. Today is just the beginning.'-StarChild
1-14-13

'Take time today to reflect on what is important to you. How are you structuring your life to achieve what is in your highest interest? Every thought you think is a choice. Be happy, think love and be light. You know what you are to do. Just do it. Today.'-StarChild 1-11-13

'Nurture yourself today. It is important to take care of yourself, body, mind, spirit and soul. Take the time to give of yourself to yourself, so that you may remember how holy you are. When you truly know that and treat yourself accordingly, you can give to others abundantly from your depth of spirit without depletion. Love yourself, love others, and be that love that shifts all. Remember only love is real, and by nurturing yourself you nurture all. Smile and be kind and full of love, for it reflects back to you and all others a thousand fold. Be you.'-StarChild 1-8-13

'Routine matters are anything but routine. Remember that each and every act you do, whether for service, for pleasure, for work or for fun is a measure of your spiritual focus. Each day is an opportunity to focus on what matters to you – where you put your energy and intentions. When you routinely send out love and peace to the world around you it comes back ten fold, and blesses you. That is the rule of the multi-verse. What are you putting out there today?'-StarChild 1-7-13

*****2012***

'It is time to act on the messages you have received. You know what you are to do. Do not wait. The time is now, go and take action to make it happen. You are being guided as to the direction to proceed. Go and bless the world with your gifts – that is why you have them. Start today to make your dreams come true. We are here to help, call on us and we will show you the way.'-StarChild 11-12-12

As you walk through this doorway know your essence is forever altered and freed from that which has prevented humanity from going forth. You are ready. Walk in courage and in love.
11-11-13

"Today is the most divine of days. The vibration of shifting of the balance of power to one of equality, generosity, compassion, kindness and respect are in place. The healing is occurring all over this planet and wholeness is being restored. Star family from all over the multiverse are here to assist you during this most auspicious time of ascension. You are becoming pure light and embodying the essence of pure love. We rejoice as we see you coming together in love to help each other and honor your planet. We smile and we see you learn and grow each day as your DNA is upgraded and you begin to use the new abilities you have been given. The shift is here, and your world will be a different place from here on. We are always here to help you, and you can call on us at anytime. You are becoming more and more telepathic, so you are hearing us as well. Soon you will have the eyes to see us too.'StarChild
11-11-12

'The balance of give and take is at play today. Sometimes it is necessary to clean out that which is no longer useful and to streamline your mode of living. When needs and wants are clearly delineated, it becomes very clear what is useful and what is fluff. Sometimes humans are very attached to 'things' and that may cause a pain when those things leave. Realize that everything is energy, and the energy of growth often requires change, whether you want the change or not. As we move through this ascension process, release in love that which is no longer part of you, and embrace the new that is coming. Go without fear in to the unknown, for you are chartering new territory. Remember than only love is real, and as such, the path is unfolding that will serve your highest good, even if it may not seem apparent at the moment. Look for the small blessings and be thankful for each one. One day it will make sense when you can see the complete picture.'-StarChild
11-2-12

'Know that where you put your will and your thoughts, therein lies your reality. Therefore, align your will with that of the divine, and all will be well. Look at the good, and shift those vibrations into one of wholeness and vibrancy. The new reality is emerging, how you think determines how it goes, so think with the mindset of love, kindness and compassion, and watch as the new world emerges.'-StarChild
10-29-12

'The intensity of yesterday continues with the remaining little bits streaming off. You should feel lighter knowing that your vibration is being honed and more in alignment with your true essence. As a star being here on Earth, you are awakening to your own nature of light. Sometimes it comes in ways that are different than you might imagine it would be, but it is always the right way at the right time, even if it may not seem like it at the time. Know you are growing and maturing in your spirituality, and as such, are being gifted with more and more encounters that are finding their way to you. Some of them are even on your media for you to see, for humans trust their eyes often times more than their gut. Learn to know with your gut, you will then see even more with your spiritual sight, bringing together the next phase of your development in ascension.'-StarChild
10-26-12

'Today is a day of intense swords. Sharp energies to hone the truth and set you free are abundant in the lineup today. Define your truth – that which is important to you – and remove from your field that which does not support that. Stand strong. You know you are love, strength, truth, beauty, joy, abundance and happiness. Resonate with that in the way that is most appropriate to you at this time. You are calling in the new way, leave the garbage behind and bring in the light of love, joy and purity. This makes a world that is consistent with your vibrations. As your vibrations have been changing throughout the ascension process, your needs, too, have changed. Know what they are, and stand strong in your truth. Your world is changing accordingly.'-StarChild 10-25-12

'Take care of your physical vessel for it houses your spirit. Feed it the proper fuel and make sure it has all that it needs – rest, shelter, clean air and water, meditation, exercise, love. Love is all that is real and your physical body is love too. Love all the little things about it – from the way the toes dig into the sand to the noises it makes to the miraculous way the blood is pumped to every organ, every minute of every day. Your body is a fantastic example of working together for the good of all. The foot does not say "I am more important than the hand because I carry you from here to there" or the heart say "I am more important than the brain because without me you can't think" – no – every part works together in the great interplay of the physical vessel you inhabit. This is to show you the way of the multiverse – everything works together, no matter how

disconnected it may appear. Love your body, love your mind, love your spirit, and treat them all with kindness, love and respect for they house 'you' in this incarnation of your spirit. Be good to yourself today.'-StarChild
10-24-12

'Intention comes in many forms, a wish, a prayer a dream – a longing in the heart that just doesn't stop. What separates intent from fantasy is that your intent is very real. The universe hears your intentions and conspires to make it happen. That is why it is so important to be clear in your intentions and in your dealing with yourself and others. Be positive. If you are continuously negative, the vibration you send to the universe is one of negativity, hence the lessons to learn. If your intentions are of the highest nature, with pure love and no attachment to the outcome, it is much easier for those intentions to take a pleasurable form. Rarely is the intention manifested in the exact form you may think it should take. Be grateful for what is, even those experiences which are 'negative', for you have created that too. Those experiences can teach us how to do things differently the next time, and to call in different energies. Be love, be light and be joy. What you radiate is what you will create. If your intention is joy, peace and love, with no attachment to the outcome, you will manifest in love that which is in your best interest for your soul at his particular time, even if it is not yet apparent. Be grateful and full of love and watch the miracles in your life occur.'-StarChild 10-23-13

'Evolution comes in many forms. How are you evolving today? The world as you currently know it is changing before you, as you bring in the new consciousness, the new way of being. There is a tug between the old and the new, and as you keep your focus towards the love, new ways are being made to hold the energy and shift the entire multiverse. Let go of that which no longer serves and keeps you back, be free to go where your spirit leads you. As the ascension continues and your DNA is upgraded, realize your conscious evolution. You always have a choice. Evolve. Grow. Learn. It all starts now.'-StarChild
10-16-12

'Integrate the experiences of your Star family contact into your physical form today. The attributes of grace, love and beauty are yours – embody them. Vibrational wholeness comes from doing your spiritual work. Let go of that which is not part of you, and embrace that which is. Merge in to the Divine Light of Consciousness and know that you are perfect just the way you are. Be kind and shift this world into love, for love is all that is real. The shift is here.'–StarChild
10-11-12

'Your consciousness is awake – you have only to free it from the bondage of fear and take the path of courage to realize all you have ever wanted is available to you. Remember that you are an unlimited being, you can do anything you truly choose (including not to do it) for the power of your mind is great. It commands your thoughts and actions and connects you to dimensions that you are now beginning to comprehend. Be free, be love and be aware. The Light is here and you are part of it. You are unlimited in your potential. Be open and experience that contact that is available to guide you. Your star family is here – now. You can find their guidance through opening your spiritual eyes and through your intuition. It is all love, and it is all good.'-StarChild
10-10-12

'Create the bridges today to connect to that which empowers you. Unhook your mind from the falsities that you have pretended to believe, and instead resonate with that which you know to be true in your soul. You are ascending, daily you are going through the process of becoming more fully you, more aligned, more congruent with your inner knowing. No fear, only freedom. Be the love and the change you wish to see, for you are creating it right now.'-StarChild
10-4-12

'Evolution of humanity is happening at an accelerated pace to prepare you for the next steps to come. It is time to unhook your mind from your brain and train your thoughts to envision the future. You are growing in multiple ways as you search for your true home. As you look to the skies, you have a knowingness that resonates true in your being. We make connection everyday in some way, shape or form. By opening your mind to the magnitude of the contact, you will begin to see us everywhere. Every living being has a consciousness, and the animation of that consciousness is love. So when you send out a loving vibration, the entire multiverse connects with you and enhances that vibe. This is the way of ascension, leave behind that which no longer serves and merge with the loving presence of all that is. You are already changing and growing. You are evolving.'-StarChild
10-3-12

'The theme to day continues with protection, love and healing. Know that you are exactly where you are supposed to be. Yes, challenging things are occurring – but they are doing so to help you to realize what you must overcome to hone your vibration. You are on the right path, realize what your lessons are and move foreword. The core essence of your vibration will lead you to all the right choices if you listen with a pure, humble, open heart. Remember that only love is real. Be kind to others and yourself, and practice compassion in all your dealings. The world is changing and you are calling in that change. Make it pure, beautiful and full of light, and you will see the vibration raise across the universe.'-StarChild
9-29-12

'Transformation is upon all as the Earth nears the galactic center. More and more humans are awaking, and once awakened can no longer pretend to be asleep. You know there is change, you can feel the presence of the Divine everywhere, as the tipping point for the human race approaches. As the ascension continues, all are asked to look at their values and ways of being. Is it congruent with who you are and who you would like to evolve into? If not, begin today to make those changes. Humanity is on the verge of evolution into homo-luminous – the light human. This light cannot tolerate hate, greed or bigotry. The time to love is now, that is how more and more contact is made with the Divine. Your Star family is here and assisting you to be the best that you can be. You can feel the love they share with you and the messages that are being sent to you on a daily basis. See them throughout the trees, the skies, the stars, and through the eyes of other

beings. Your awakening is now, and is calling you to an ever higher level of vibration. Then you in turn can help others on their path to ascension.'-StarChild
9-25-12

Happiness
'What is the essence of your soul? How do you desire to serve humanity? All beings wish to be inservice to the light. What makes you supremely happy? That is your path. The path is happiness that blesses you and those around you, and lifts you all up together. It is important to follow the voice in your soul that leads you to divine bliss. Listen, listen, listen, for in being true to your soul, you will be made free. Some of you are doing just that, and living the life you know you were born to live. Others have a desire to change something in their life because it comes up in their field as a distortion that something is not right. Listen to the voice, choose your path, and love who you are and what you do. Only love is real, and it permeates everything in the universe. Look with your spiritual eyes to see, and give thanks for every blessing you receive.'-StarChild
9-17-12

luminosity
'The wisdom of the heavens is integrated into the Earth plane today. Be in unity, and know that all is good. Many visions, healings, and a sense of oneness and purpose permeates all. The new Earth is being formed with each thought you think, each act of kindness you perform and with every quanta of unconditional love that you exude. The seas and skies vibrate higher today, as do all the beings that resonate in between. Take the time today to notice your vibration, how has it changed? Do you feel more luminous? Notice the signs that the Earth creatures are giving, those that fly, swim, crawl, walk and run are sending the messages to you and to the others who can understand them. Honor them, and send your love to all. That is the path to peace, and you are walking it.'-StarChild
9-16-12

The time is now
'The experience of being with your Star family has initiated (or re-initiated) you in to the next phase of your evolution. Your DNA is being upgraded and your abilities enhanced. You have had all kinds of experiences, some have seen our ships, some our lights, and many have felt our presence in your hearts, but all who have contacted us we have heard. We love you all, and are excited about the changes that your love will bring about. Today is the day of the initiate, of initiating a new phase on this planet that you will create with your light and love. We will be in contact with you again tonight, and from now on, you will know when you feel our presence with you. No doubt, no fear, only love and trust. As you become more familiar with our presence with you, you will see that we have been here all along, watching over you and helping you along the roadmap of your life to steer you to where you are now. We are in every natural thing,

and will never leave you. As your DNA continues to upgrade, this will become more and more apparent to you as you ascend and evolve into homo-luminois, the light human. For now, enjoy the bliss, and remember that only love is real, all else is an illusion, and you can shape your reality in whatever way you choose. As you choose to live in peace, love and harmony you are aware of the sacredness of this journey you have chosen to undertake. You have kept your Divine appointment, and we are very happy.'-StarChild
9-15-12

'Honor who you are, where you have come from and where you are going. By paying respect to your divine essence, you become truer to your path. You are all beings of light, full of light and wonder, with a knowingness that kindness, compassion, love and peace are how to create the new Earth. Practice that compassion and love today, each quanta of love you share is magnified in the universe, and its' power heightened. Remember that only love is real, all else is an illusion. You have chosen to be here now, at this most auspicious time on Earth, to help humanity ascend to the next step in the evolution – homoluminous – the light human. As you integrate the light into your being, your spirit grows and your heart holds even more love and compassion, as you vibrate in harmonious resonance with the trees, birds, waters, skies, rocks, elementals, and all beings of all types everywhere. They day is coming soon when we show ourselves to you. Be in this luminous vibration and you shall see. Your Star family is here, and we are speaking to you through your natural world. We see your heart and know you are ready. Can you hear us already?'-StarChild 9-12-12

'Remember you are beings of unlimited creativity and wonder. Changes are happening all over the galaxy at this time, and you are being shown any old traumatic patterns that still must leave. Release, the time of harmony and peace is upon you. As you prepare for contact with our world, be of a joyful heart. Remember only love is real and that is who you are at your essence. All beings are connected via the energy and the source, which is love. This is a time of celebration, gather together and experience this with others. The rocks, plants and animals all dance with joy as well. Be of a joyful heart and connect in spirit. Watch the signs and listen to your inner voice. It is time.'-StarChild
9-11-12

'Pay homage to the great Earth mother today for she provides all your needs and keeps you grounded in the reality that you have chosen to incarnate into. Thank you to the plants, animals, waters, air, rocks, and inter-dimensional beings that vibrate in unison to make this a supportive environment for human life. You are about to make the great leap into the 5th dimension, and we are here to assist you in this endeavor. Pay homage to your Earth, your mother, and thank her for all she provides. Abundance is everywhere. The great love of the Divine has blessed you with this being on whom your very existence depends upon. We are here and we are watching, and will be with you very soon. Keep watching the signs in the skies that are being provided to you daily. Listen to the small, still voice that knows. You can feel it is coming soon. Prepare yourself.'-StarChild
9-9-12

'Spontaneous acts of beauty and kindness are joyful expressions of love. When you smile from the inside and beam that love vibration out to the world, you affect the energy field in a very positive way. Shift into kindness today, and watch the world shift with you. Every moment of every day you have a choice. Positive or negative – it is up to you. While you may not be able to change events, circumstances or people, your ability to remain positive can improve the circumstances and benefit all. Make peace your goal, beginning with inner peace – then radiate that peace to the world and create anew.'-StarChild
9-2-12

'Ground into the holy planet that is Earth today. This blessed being provides all that you need, including food, water, shelter, and the energetics that maintain the forces responsible for life, including the electromagnetic force, gravity, and the atmosphere. The Earth helps you to ground and be centered and calm. Take notice of the plants, rocks, soil; all is there to support humanity. Honor this, and be thankful. Breathe that love and gratitude back in to the Great Earth Mother and she will show you her love too.'-StarChild
9-1-12

'Be at peace. Love is all that is real, and love leads to peace. If there is not peace in your heart, then examine it to see what is blocking that vibration. All is good, do not fear, the transition is in place, and although some may be having some difficult situations, good will come out of it eventually. Be kind, love others, and find your inner peace.'-StarChild
8-30-12

'Go where your heart leads you and do not be afraid. The world is changing and you have been restless as you know that is true. Big shifts are coming, and that is why you are feeling what you are feeling. It is the preparation. Stay focused on the inner knowing, and listen for the information that is coming through. Watch the sky. Your Star family is VERY near, and the world is about to change as you now know it. Be in joyful anticipation of all that is good. The time is now. Be present.'-StarChild
8-23-12

'The Star beings, angels, fairies and elementals are calling you to remember the magic and wonder of the world around you. The moon and planets in the sky glowing with the wonder of the ages calls one to remember your true identity – that of the stars. Watch the night sky in wonder, remember your family. Watch the day sky and see the beauty and power that is present in you as well. The world you see is a reflection of that which is inside. It is a mirror. What do you see?'-StarChild 8-12-12

'Star family energies are very near today. Watch your dreams, your intuitions, and look for us in the sky. Some of you are beginning to see this reality, for some it is a knowing. You are integrating the DNA upgrade that was received last week. Some of you are having emotional upsets to clear the last remaining aspects of what has held you in bondage. Release it and integrate the love and peace that the divine has for you. This is an opportunity to grow and to hone your senses. We are near, we are here, can you see and sense us? You will soon.'-StarChild
8-10-12

'Today is one of those days to find pleasure in the ordinary things. Remember that the life here is extra ordinary – unlike any else in the universe. You chose to be here at this time so enjoy it. Simple daily tasks take on a holy meaning when one realizes that each is an act of love. Each breath breathes in the Divine, release any negativity with your exhale, and breathe in light. The transformation has begun. the star family is here, the DNA has been upgraded, and some of the light codes activated. With each new activation of light, humans are evolving in to the new human – homoluminous – human of light. Expect more inter dimensional experiences as you seek them. You are being upgraded to thrive through the shifts. You are strong and full of love and courage. Show that love to all today.'-StarChild
8-9-12

'Sometimes when one is healing, those aspects of one's self that need to be released emerge. This can be uncomfortable. Release is a powerful healing tool for transformation. Let go of people, places, things, and situations. One can only control one's response. Trust that your needs will be provided and they will be. Fear comes in many forms, so does trust. Learn to listen to that small still voice inside, which is your higher self, and align yourself with your own personal truth. This will free you from the bondage of self imposed limitation or the need to please others at the expense of oneself. Treat all with love and respect and expect that of others as well. Your truth is calling, you are free. Sometimes one does not realize that they are free and continue to act as if they are still in bondage. The Star family is here, he bondage is removed. Act accordingly.'-StarChild
8-8-12

'Today is a day of action. Channel that energy into productive practical endeavors, for the next few days will be intense. Prepare yourself physically, emotionally and spiritually. Be ready to remove that which has been holding you in bondage, you are about to be free! Be full of joy as you prepare, clean, drum, rattle, smudge, and anticipate the new energy of total freedom. Your Star family is very near, and very soon you will feel them, sense them and some will even see them! This is the most auspicious time.'-StarChild
8-1-12

'The message for today is one of trust. Trust that each event in your life has been getting you ready for today. Great things are on the horizon that will change your life forever. Open your heart, look to the sky, breathe in the Earth, soon all will be revealed. It is the most auspicious time to be on Earth.'-StarChild
7-31-12

'Are you ready for your Star family to greet you? It is happening very soon. Prepare and open your heart in love, gratitude and anticipation. Be full of kindness and compassion. Remember to walk in peace. The new earth is being created with loving vibrations. Be ready and aware, for you are creating it too.'-StarChild
7-30-12

'Today is a reminder from the universe to appreciate the power of joy and gratitude in your life. When one is connected to the divine, the natural flow is joy into gratitude and back into joy. This flow between joy and gratitude is inextricably linked to the positive current that flows through one's life, breathing life into the thought forms that arise to manifest those creations which are in your highest good. See the divine in everything, and be joyful and appreciative. This will keep you in the high vibrations necessary to continue the ascension process.'-StarChild 7-28-12

'You are being asked today to take a good look at those patterns which still hold you back. Trace their root and find the origin of the thought form. It is time to let it go. Wounds from your childhood shape who you are and help one to develop coping patterns. Once an adult, one must look at those coping patterns and honor them for their teachings, and for keeping you safe, and if they no longer serve your growth, let them go. You are safe and protected in love from the divine. Remember that only love is real, and when certain patterns arise it is because you are ready to let them go, and be free. The Divine has said to let go of your bondage. It is time. Your star family is here to help. Connect in spirit and go within, the answers are all there.'-StarChild
7-27-12

'Remember always that you are in service to the light. Light beings from the stars surround you to assist you on your appointed path. Walk in service and in love, and all tasks you do, no matter how big or how small, take on a divine presence. Everything you do matters – everything. Every thought, word, action, and deed. When one is in divine harmony, life flows. Take time today to ponder and reflect on how you approach your life. Is it divine service? Remember only love is real. Walk in harmony, light and love.'-StarChild 7-26-12

'The experiences of the past help one to see the current situation through those filters. Incarnations are a series of lessons from birth to death, and many of you are witnessing those transitory phases in life now. Your roots nourish you as you grow through this time on earth. When you are born there are a set of challenges to overcome and blessings to discover. When you transit to the other side with death, you are released from bondage and the only thing you take with is love. A life review shows how you have or have not loved in certain situations, or if you have abused your gifts or used them wisely. You return to the state of love and light which is the true state of being. Resentment, anger and fear melt away, as the human suit is discarded in favor of pure spirit. Remember you are a spirit who is here in a body, but you are not your body. The consciousness that animates you comes from Source and is pure. Remember that always as you encounter vibrations that challenge who you are. Only love is real. The vibratory transits are happening very fast as the ascension progresses. Remember your roots are always in light, grow accordingly.'-StarChild 7-25-12

'Accept your gifts. Move forward and acknowledge your part in this ascension process. Breathe and connect deep into the mother Earth, thank her for holding you on this planet as you grow, and realize that all your needs are provided for. Remember to be happy and shift your vibration through your talents. It is this alignment with source that changes the world. Be the change.'-StarChild
7-23-12

'Powerful transformative energies at work today. This time period is very effective at looking at your life and seeing what you want to keep, and what you want to change. A time of great growth is at hand, and all are feeling the effects one way or another. Perhaps you have been more restless lately? Perhaps a new opportunity has recently arisen? Check your intuition, perhaps this is the opportunity you have been calling in with all your recent transformations! This is a period of shaking off the old ways and adopting the new. This is not always as easy path, but it is necessary for your spiritual growth. As you continue to release old patterns and redefine what is important, you will notice that your vibration becomes more purely you. That is how it should be. By being more purely you, you will attract that which is in your best interest, for the alignment of the energies will be compatible. Gain the confidence in yourself to see these changes, and how they have been made

manifest in your life. How has the recent time period of the last two earth years been for you? What changes have you noticed? You are in the ascension and that growth is swift and profound. Notice today how you have grown. Give thanks that you are coming into your pure vibration. It is good. It is all good. Even that which appears to not be good, is good, for it teaches you what you no longer want to create. Be love, be joy and be thankful. The best is yet to come.'-StarChild
7-20-12

'After yesterday's chaotic energies, today is a day to rest and nurture. Nap, swim, take a bath, cry, do whatever you need to do to nurture yourself today. Bring that love and that nurturing into your field for all today. Love the plants, the animals, the sky the sea, for it is all one. The energies run chaotically as they draw out that which is no longer needed to make room for the new growth. That can sometimes leave humans a little raw emotionally. By giving yourself the nurturing you need, or by allowing others to nurture you if that feels appropriate, you allow the healing, growth and integration of those energies. Each morphic field that the Earth passes through contains the energies of the stars, and with it, the growth that accompanies it. During this time of ascension, integrate that energy with the love of the divine that is always present. The movement of the differing energies creates a current of growth that is essential to the process. It wipes away stagnation and allows the verdant growth of the soul to occur. Nurture that growth today, there are other days for action. Today be the love you share with others, just remember to give it to yourself as well.'-StarChild 7-17-12

'Remember your own worth. All is connected to the same source. That life giving force animates you and makes you who you are. Remember that all your need will always be provided for, and that there is abundance and beauty all around. Your body has sprung from the earth, connecting you to the ways of this planet. See the divine in all creation, including yourself, and vibrate with the knowingness that you are beautiful and full of grace. Abundance is everywhere, by tuning your sensors to one of thanksgiving and being truly grateful for all that you have, you will see how abundant your life is. What you focus on is what you will also create, so focus on appreciating all that is in your life. Your perspective will change, and then often so will your surroundings. Remember only love is real. When you live that, you will see that. Love, trust and appreciation are all from source. Always remember you are loved and your star family is near.'-StarChild
7-13-12

'All is in divine right order. It might seem as there is too much to do, or not enough time, or this or that, but in reality it is all progressing just the way it should. Lessons are being learned, finishing touches are being polished, and new endeavors are being created. The being called Earth that you live upon provides the structure for all of your needs. She is the very manifestation of life, upon which all matter in this world is created. By utilizing the creative force on this planet, you are learning the lessons of harnessing cohesive light into a structure. The choices that you make to live your life set up a vibrational stream that conspires to make those choices come to fruition. By allowing that creative force to be bathed in the power of love, you bring joy into your life and set you further upon your path you chose when you first came to this planet. You are creative, manifesting beings, your thoughts are very powerful for they create. As you consciously create in love, peace and harmony you will notice synchronistic happenings that occur on a regular basis. There is balance and timing to this great cycle, and it is reflective of your energy that you put into it. Where are you in the cycle?-StarChild 7-12-12

'Self knowledge comes from careful introspection in the quiet of your soul. Listen inside to the what calls your spirit, it will always be love. If there is a snag in your aura, or a density in your spirit you will feel a drain on the love inside. Heal that by showing yourself love and forgiveness and filling the area with light. Get up and move around to shake the energy into balance if you need to. Happiness is the natural state of the human. When all is in balance the joy is there. Many of you are going through great changes in this time of the ascension. Listen to your heart and have the courage to make those changes that are appropriate for you at this time. Know yourself. You are a child of the stars and by following your intuition you will be led exactly where you are supposed to be. Acknowledge and be grateful for your gifts for they make you who you are. Be happy and bask in the vibration of joy that is your birthright. There is love all around, even where there is sorrow or loss. The trick is in learning to find the love in all situations and to stay in your balance while doing so. Even tears contain beauty and love as they cleanse your soul and remove impurities. Know who you are and how you process. With that knowledge you will gain the understanding of how you relate and create. Remember that only love is real, and that by keeping your column of light clear, you will be able to tap into your essence more clearly.'-StarChild 7-10-12

'Spontaneous acts of beauty come from love and gratitude. The illusion of time is being seen for what it is, and the time tables you are used to dealing with no longer apply. Those changes that occur are taking less of the perceived 'time' to happen, and as you flow with the spontaneity of the vibration of now, you will resonate with that deep beauty that leads to wonderful adventures, spiritual awakening and fun. The prodding you feel to move, change jobs, get married, divorced, or any other major change is amplified during this time of increased vibrational amplification. Trust the guidance of the divine, and go for what you know to be true for you in your heart. It is an expression of love and truth to follow your heart's path. Wonderful rewards await those that follow their heart, it might leave a few scars as well, but they will be remembered with honor. Call forth that sacred part of you that knows to come forward and sing, dance and create in joy the life that is waiting for you. Your star family is here guiding you, calling you to your true destiny. Listen and be at peace as you hear your true heartbeat of the stars.'-StarChild 7-9-12

'Take time to acknowledge the blessed waters of the land. All of the waters are interconnected, including the water of your own body. The vibrational message that you encode your body and the land with is received and amplified via the water. When you remember to appreciate from the very depth of your soul the water and all that it is attached to, a profound gratitude will appear. That profound gratitude is what drives the creation process for your highest good. Love, trust and appreciation are three of the highest vibrations of love. So remember to be in those vibrations to flow in the river of love. Love is the only thing that returns to you more than give out, to amplify that wavelength through the cosmos. Your star family has imprinted this love in to you so that you may love others. Remember that only love is real. Appreciate those gifts, say thank you and love all.'-StarChild
7-7-12

'Consideration of others goes a long way. Please, thank you, I'm sorry (if needed and true), and how can I help are phrases that can smooth over misunderstandings and align the vibrations again. When the vibrations are out of balance, it is necessary to examine why and how to prevent that from happening again. Words carry great vibrational power, so use them mindfully and with integrity. Thoughtlessness leads to much unnecessary misunderstandings. Being mindful in your words and actions prevents those misunderstandings and allows the proactive manifesting force to create more easily. Be kind and compassionate, connect in love and be joy.'-StarChild
7-6-12

'Is there any disturbance in your field? If so, look inside to see if the healing power of forgiveness needs to be applied to your life. Forgiveness does not mean that you blindly accept the situations or people who have perpetuated the actions, but rather that you release them from your energy field and from playing the role of abuser or victim with you. That will free you to fully encompass the joy and the love that is your natural state of being. Have you been the abuser? Then forgive yourself. Have you been the victim? then also forgive yourself, along with the abuser. You have decided to incarnate here to learn these lessons. Those who have taught you forgiveness through their abusive actions towards you are fulfilling their role until you learn that lesson and change the

energetic stream. Let them go from your field and watch how free you feel without them in it. Choose to walk in love and light and be no longer held hostage by those thought forms. Free yourself. Forgiveness is the key, compassion the way, and courage the vibration. Walk in love and light and be free to choose a path that makes you happy.'-StarChild
7-5-12

'There is healing in the cellular memories of all cells. All that has been alive – including those fossilized into stone – contain valuable information that is available to you if you seek it. The vibrations that are stored there are encoded. As you grow in your vibrations, you gain access to those higher codes of knowledge. They are always there, just your ability to perceive them is heightened with prayer and meditation, as well as activation. The star gates are opened and the information is there for you. Go and seek it and be as one with your star family. Go to those places in nature that vibrate high for you – there is a message that will indicate the next step on your path. Remember only love is real, and to love and appreciate each gift on your path. Some may not agree with you – and that is okay – be true to the longings in your soul and step up on to your divine path. That is why you are here.'-StarChild
7-3-12

'Ground into the Earth mother those excess energies you are carrying around. Today is a day of joy and celebration. Give Earth your blessings for she gives you hers. You carry the energies of your star family – sometimes that makes it more difficult to ground, so make it a point to breathe the love into the earth and also from the earth into you to harmonize those energies and to strengthen you. You came here to serve and protect her, so honor her with that love. With each gift from the bounty of nature you are being reminded that all needs will always be met. Each bird, flower, animal, and cloud is a reminder that all is in divine harmony. Resonate with that divine harmony and notice the depth of simplicity that nature applies.

Incorporate that simplicity into your life and you will see just how rich the experience of being alive can be. Focus on appreciating the little things. Remember to say thank you and to be kind, and watch as the vibrations of love and light permeate everything to make you even happier than you are right now.'-StarChild
7-2-12

'It is time to see the true level of reality that is all around you. Many beings from many other dimensions are all around you, helping and guiding you. The plant and animal beings are great teachers on this earth plane, listen to them and they will teach you the wonders of the universe. Subtle impressions, dreams, and knowing-ness are some of the ways that those from the other realms 'talk' to you to help you on your path. Listen with all your senses, including your intuition, to guide you as you prepare for contact. This is becoming more and more important as we begin this new time period of light and love. The unspoken is more powerful than that which is verbalized. Be very aware of your vibrations that you put out. Be love and light on all levels, and you will find that those other beings guidance comes through even more clear to help you. Wisdom and understanding will be gained from them. Prepare yourself.'-StarChild
6-29-12

'You are a divine reflection of spirit. Health and enlightenment allow one to carry a higher vibration while here on the earth plane. Today is a day to reflect upon your earthly vehicle. Prayer, meditation, clean foods, pure water and clean air all contribute to healthy frame of mind, which leads to a healthy soul. Whatever you immerse yourself in is that which you will become. Choose that which supports your health, for in so doing, you will vibrate higher. You are still integrating the Christ light that came, and therefore careful attention to your physical body is necessary. Choose those foods which the your higher self resonates with. Each cell has a consciousness, and when you acknowledge that consciousness in all things everywhere, including the foods you ingest, you are more easily able to

manifest that which is for your highest good. Your star family is here to help you. Remember only love is real, so love yourself and feed and exercise the body that houses your soul. As you do so, the integration of the energies will become easier and you will vibrate higher.'-StarChild
6-27-12

'Today is a day of rest. Nurture yourself today. Be with the element of water and let things flow. Take a swim or a bath, cry if you need release, but let the watery essence flow today with compassion, truth and love. Feel the vibe of those you love, remember to tell them that you love them, for those words hold great vibrational power. Be in that power of unconditional love. It is the new way, and it is now.'-StarChild 6-26-12

'As the moment of the gift draws near, random acts of kindness and spontaneous joyful laughter will become more common. The light is coming and all will be affected by this great event. Open your heart for all are connected, the plants, animals, humans, galactic beings, light forms, and much more. Your ascension is here, feel the vibration that has been building over the past week. All are connected to each other through the breath, through the light, and through the love. Love one another, be kind, and let compassion be in your heart. Be joyful, your star family is here, the ships are near, and you are loved.'-StarChild
6-22-12

'The breath connects all beings together in the morphic soup of consciousness. Wind is the breath of the Earth. Wind cleanses, refreshes, creates and sometimes destroys to make way for the new. The mental capacities of human are of the wind element, while the emotional element is water. Wind is water in its freest state, like respiration of trees or an exhalation. So the water and the air are complementary forces. So it is with the beings on the Earth. Are you cleansing, destroying or creating? Are you connecting your breath with the wind that is all around you? What are you learning from it? How does it affect you? Can you feel the trace of the water element with each breeze? As you breathe in each breath – is it you breathing in or the divine breathing

out? There is connection between all the worlds. Concentrate on that with each breath. The evolution is occurring, with a three level jump in just a few days. Meditate on that while you breathe the divine breath in holy union with all other beings, such as your star family, the animals and the plants of this world and the Agarthians. All is connected with breath and with love. Breathe that into your field and watch and listen to the stillness of change.'-StarChild
6-19-12

'Intent is a powerful force for creation and manifestation of our purest vibrational essence. Creator will always give you what you want in your heart. If you need to learn lessons you will receive those lessons, remember that you asked to learn them on some level. When you are in the flow joyful manifestations occur due to the alignment of divine right will. When you create from an ego basis, your creations will not be fulfilling. Remember that you are light and love and to be in that vibration always. Feel that essence in your belly to manifest that in your highest good and that is in the best interests of others as well. Be happy for you have created your life, you can create a whole different life if you wish as well. You power to manifest is much stronger than you realize, or you would create situations to further your vibrational essence of love more easily. So begin today to listen to the vibration of love that you are and to manifest from that place of pure love and divine intent. That is how to bring in the new Earth through this ascension process.'-StarChild 6-16-12

'Abundance is all around you. Look to Earth, for she provides all you need. Do not wish ill upon those that have what you think that you want, instead, strive for your own happiness, and wish others well. Look at your own abundance and life path, do not compare. Look to see if you are blocking your abundance with your vibration – and if so – shift it into what is in your high heart – pure love. You are love and light, and as such should vibrate as high as possible. Be love, for that is all that is real, then you all find true joy in other's happiness as well a your own. Remember, love is all that is real.'-StarChild
6-12-12

'Every day is a new beginning. Honor where you have been, for all those experiences have made you who you are today. Love those who have been unkind to you, for they have shown you how to be compassionate and how to forgive. Forgiveness leads to love and since love is all that is real, there is no need to hold on to bitterness, anger or regret. Today is a new day, be in the vibration of love and utilize that in this pacha (time cycle) that has just begun. It is the time cycle of meeting your essence again. That essence is love and light. Remember that as you go through your day. Bless the beings everywhere you go and watch as they, in turn will bless other beings, turning in to the cycle of blessings that drive the creative force on Earth. Watch as

the healing occurs spontaneously and effortlessly when all is in right alignment with divine purpose. Are you aligned with your divine purpose? The time is now. Your Star family is here to help and guide you through every step. Breathe deep and know that you are loved more than you can even imagine. You are full of courage and strength, that is why you are here. And you are never alone, the Holy One is always with you. Remember this always and draw on the strength that will see you through anything. Be love, be light and be blessed.'-StarChild
6-7-12

'The new time cycle is here! As the heavenly bodies aligned and Venus transited the sun, the shift occurred that has ushered in a time of new beginnings. As prophesied through many traditions, the age of light and love is here and now. It may take a while for the physical aspect to catch up to the energetic presence that occurred yesterday, and many of your felt this most auspicious shift happening. Shed any patterns that no longer serve you, and emerge into the new you along with the new Earth and the new consciousness. Release, forgive and heal as you go forth in this new day. You are purity and light. Go forth in to the world and bless everyone and everything you see today. Remember that only love is real and that love is transferable when you love

others and project that love into the world. That is how to shift. Many in the world are full of fear, transcend that and show them the way of love. You are the way showers, the ones who know. Your Star family is here to love and guide you. Purify your essence. Bless the world and watch as you, too, are blessed in return.'-StarChild
6-6-12

'Clarity of thought is what is called for today. Be clear in your intention so that you may flow with the creative force. As Earth comes closer to the galactic center, the intensity of the spirit grows stronger. Be clear in how you are to grow through this shift. As the new earth is created, the thought forms that you bring lay the groundwork for the future. Be of right mind, full of integrity, light and love and watch as your future comes in alignment with those thoughts. You have more power in your thoughts that many of you realize, for you truly do create your own reality. The more clear you are in doing so, the easier this will continue to be.'-StarChild
6-3-12

'Remember to always speak your truth. Others may not agree or like what you have to say, but you will be free. Do not be intimidated by manipulative techniques that come from low vibration source. You come from the stars and a such, should vibrate high and in love. Always check your information inside your soul, for the vibrational resonance of truth will always show you what is in your highest good. There is a lot of misinformation in this 3 dimensional world, you must use your ability to decipher to seek out your truth. Love those that criticize for they know no other way to deal with their pain. Bring the highest vibration of love to all beings everywhere, so that all may live in love and peace. Transcend the ego and live from source.'
6-1-12

Honor
'Honor all beings. Those that inhabit the earth especially, are sensitive to the thought forms that shape the 3 dimensional reality. It is time to recreate and reclaim the Earth, and care for her the way she deserves. She gives life, and through the waters this planet makes a habitat suitable for humanity. The greed, lust, manipulation and ugliness of humans has caused the vibration to lower, thus it is of utmost importance to change those thought forms and vibrate higher. Many of you are already doing just that. The very life of the planet Earth depends upon this. Remember that only love is real; the vibration of love is healing and restorative. Send those loving vibrations to the Earth mother to help

her restore. Even the little things count; pick up trash, recycle and reuse items, eat and grow your food organically. This perpetuates a cycle of restoration. Star family is here to help you. You have only to close your eyes and meditate to feel them. They are all around. The divine connection is in everything. Even that which appears 'ugly' is but a cry for love. The Agarthians are now partnering with certain humans to help in this restoration. Their very existence is inter-dependent with that of the Earth. All worlds are interdependent. It is one of the reasons a healthy ecosystem contains a balance. You, too, must be in balance. Balance in love.'-StarChild 5-31-12

A new day has begun
'Take stock of your inner knowledge and growth. Your family from the stars are here to help. Since April 27, 2012, human time, the Agarthians have been available to help people who have the high vibration. They are available to partner with humans to aide in the ascension process. The vibrations of humans from the past had vibrated so low that it put the very Earth herself in danger. They have come to heighten the vibration of humanity to raise the frequency of the entire earth. We are all connected. All the worlds are connected. What happens in the earth plane affects all worlds simultaneously. Be mindful of your thoughts, words and deeds. Make them congruent with love and light and the world will indeed vibrate higher and the results will be a happier, healthier world with highly vibrating beings ushering in the new earth.'-StarChild
5-30-12

'Experience, integrate and release. That is how humans learn and grow. Today marks a special transition through a star gate through the ring of fire. Listen inside for insights as to how to proceed from here. The ascension process is here, and another 'jump' in the energy will be felt by those sensitive enough to quiet their mind and listen. Integrate this energy into your being; this is star energy coming through. Continue to release any emotional attachments that are binding you to your past and distorting your emotional body. Remember only love is real. Holding on to dysfunctional patterns is not love. See the beauty of your world with appreciative eyes, and watch as it transforms around you. You create your reality, what are you creating today?'-StarChild
5-20-12

'Transformation is coming, the star gate is opening and the ascension process is in full swing. Prepare for this today with prayer and meditation, and the knowingness of who you are. You have been getting downloaded with the information of who you truly are. Have you honored that? These past times have been to hone you into the being that you are at your core essence. Emotions have come up to give you understanding, and to let go of that which no longer serves, and to transform it into love and forgiveness. This is how the new Earth is called in. Honor and know that you play and important part with each vibration you put into the matrix of consciousness. Keep the vibrations high level, honor yourself, other beings, and your Earth. The time is very near, these next two

earth days will test and hone you. Be ready for what may come to challenge you, for it is only an illusion to make you a better person. The ascension is here, you are watched over and guided, and loved more than you can ever remember in your human state. Be that love and you will be that change.'-StarChild
5-19-12

'The theme of creating your reality continues today. The beings of the inner earth are helping you as well. Soon the world you see will be different from how it is now, and you are responsible for what that change is in your life. Look to the future with courage and strength, and realize that there are no mistakes, only learning experiences. Each day as Earth comes closer to the galactic center, the prophesied changes are occurring. You are a part of that. As you create in love and light, realizing that you are pure spirit, the new Earth emerges. The energies may make it feel like you are being squeezed then released, this is to help you integrate the new energies that come every day as part of the ascension process. Integrate this into your being. Your star family is here to help, you have only to tune in to find them.'-StarChild
5-18-12

'Creation and destruction are opposite ends of the same vibrational frequency. One must often destroy aspects of one's life to move on to the new with elegance and grace, no longer bound by the constraints of the past. The new earth is being created, but the destruction of the old ways is also part of the cycle now. Is there anything that you are holding on to that is no longer of service to your spiritual well being? Change is happening, and as Earth reaches closer to the galactic center, more changes will come. This can be a wonderful process of new beginnings, but only if you have released that which no longer serves you. You are called to live in integrity, love and peace. The element of today is fire. Fire cleanses and transmutes. What do you need to

transmute today? The time is now. The veil is thinning and the new earth is upon you. Be who you are from the vibrational essence of your soul. You are perfect in your essence. Burn away the chaff and keep the good stuff, you are bringing in the new. Be love, for only love is real, and if a trial by fire is necessary, give thanks, for it is for your own highest growth to be the best that you can be. As you continue to pare down to your soul essence, you will find the changes freeing, and will look forward to more. Courage replaces any fear, and gives birth to a new way of life. You are loved more than you can ever imagine. Look for those signs of love everywhere, and you will begin to see.'StarChild
5-17-12

'Intention is the vibration of the day. The color is yellow. How you manifest is determined upon your intent. Be clear, just and full of love. Create your divine intention to be light, love and peace. The new earth is being created with these frequencies. Activate your third eye and see with the light of spirit to guide you in your manifestations. Do what is good for others, but in alignment with your vibration and the changes will occur. The beings on this planet are helping you to bring in this light, as is your galactic family. Create in light and love. Be mindful of the signs from the winged ones today, for they are not only watching you – but showing you the way.'-StarChild 5-15-12

'Nurture yourself today in the arms of the great Earth mother. She provides all that you need. Remember to give thanks to this wonderful being, and to all the beings, those that nurture you, those that you nurture, for you all help each other in this great ascension process. Relax today, enjoy and just be. The flow will take you where you are to be, so don't push, don't rush, slow down and enjoy the ride. Take time to appreciate all that you have in your life, health, family, friends, clean water, pure air, and all the beings that surround you – those you can see and those you cannot. As you appreciate the mysteries you will be gifted with the ability to see more, and appreciate more. Love, trust and appreciation are vibrations to live in. You will find peace as you tune into these vibrations. Remember that only love is real, and that your Star family is with you always.'-StarChild
5-13-12

'Today is a day of joy and celebration. Some of you may be able to see those beings of the other realms, such as faeries, angels and elementals today. Embrace with oneness the activation of the higher chakras. Give thanks to all creation for it is all a blessing. The rocks, trees, water, sun, earth, sky, humans, plants, animals, and other living beings sing in joy today. You are ascending, and as such, the vibrations that used to be beyond your reach are now available to you. Be in appreciation of all creation, for not only are you are a part of it, you help to create it. The vibrations you send out create your world, so create with loving vibrations full of light. You are creating the new Earth with each thought, word and deed. Be compassion, love and light, and as you continue to ascend, you will be rewarded with more of that yourself. Love, trust and appreciation are the vibrations of the ones you call angels. Perhaps you will catch a glimpse of them today.'-StarChild
5-12-12

'Today the new Earth moves forward into ascension. Forgiveness and release are the keys to help you to ascend along with it. There is no need to hold on to the old patterns of victim or abuser, they are all experiences to teach you how to live, love and heal. Look inward today, is there any lingering anger or resentment inside you? Release it and be free from the bondage of self inflicted pain. You are free to be who you truly are - beings of light. There is only love, accept that and move through into the bliss. The great mountain has spoken, your Star family is here and the waters sparkle with the vibration of love, cleansing and healing. Enjoy today, transform and be light, and remember that you are loved more than you could ever know.'-StarChild
4-29-12

'Honor your dreams – the messages from the divine that provide information and inspiration to your life. Respect them and watch as the divine manifestation of your innermost desires are fulfilled. As we proceed through this awakening process, many dreams are coming, some are explored, realized and done, others are seeping into your heart to make changes to honor the vibration that you incarnated on this planet with. The time to honor your vibration is now. Listen to your dreams they provide you with the template of how to manifest your destiny. Often there will be communication with your Star family to help clarify and point you in the right direction. The rules have changed, you are now free to manifest your destiny

according to the love vibration you incarnated here with. Be love and live in faith that you are on the right path. Your dreams signal the path that you are to take. Listen and be thankful for the divine is always guiding you towards your highest path, even if it may not seem like it at the time. When you get to the top of the metaphorical mountain, you will see how the path that got you there was the perfect one for you. Sometimes there are looping paths before you find your way through. This too is important for your ascension. Release the need to loop, and go forward, ever towards you ascension. Live in courage, love and faith, and know that you are loved beyond measure.'-StarChild
4-22-12

'Sometimes emotions can cause doubt about your path. This serves to teach you to examine your heart – to see where it truly lies. Trauma has both the ability to cleanse or to harm the choice is in how you handle it. Use it to grow and purify your path so you contain light and love – not anger or bitterness. Sometimes truths hurt and sometimes they will set you free, and some times they are not truths at all, but all serve for your highest growth potential. Earth is a challenging school at times and you have all come here to learn how to love. Transcend and know that only love is real, all else is illusion, even your suffering is an illusion brought upon attachment to an idea, person, place or thing. Transcend and thank all that is for showing you yet another way to love. Appreciate the lesson and live and love in peace.'-StarChild 4-17-12

"Today is a day of rest and integration. Much has been happening and many of you still need a rest to heal your bodies and integrate the new frequencies that have been downloaded. You star family is near, some of you will experience their presence, especially in about two weeks in earth time from now when some of the beings from other dimensions are scheduled for contact. Be aware for messages through the natural world and through dreams. Prepare yourself and your surroundings for this contact. Purify and cleanse for this is a holy encounter. Be ready for the next level, for it is near. Remember that love is all that is real, so seek resolution, kindness and compassion; be one with the vibration of love and appreciation. The time is now.'-StarChild
4-15-12

Love

'Star gates are open as is the bridge in you to connect to them. Know that you can travel astrally to any plane if you have the awareness to do so. From there you can see that what you have created is orchestrated according to your own personal lesson for life, with joy and bliss thrown in once you understand the gift of the lesson. There is no need for suffering, that is a human condition, you have the power to choose happiness. Your star family is always there watching you with loving eyes. Soon you will see them and as the veil continues to thin, others may as well. Be true to the mission, love one another, and remember the only thing that is true or lasting is love.'-StarChild 4-4-12

'Today is another day of soul transformation. Expect some old emotional issues to come to the surface along with the ability to look into the yourself for insight as to how to transcend this pattern and be free from it. Purity in spirit is what is called for, for this is pure love and in pure love there is no pain. Be ready to love and forgive and release to the universe that which no longer serves. As the ascension process continues to purify your spirit, begin to realize those more childlike aspects that you came into existence in this earth-plane with. Laughter, joy, and spontaneity are just some of the more playful aspects of your human-ness. Just as a child loves from their spirit and plays from their heart, so you too should find a way to be spontaneously creative just for the shear joy of it. In joy you transform and create the new reality.'-StarChild 3-31-12

'Today's message is about connection. Many humans only think in 3d. The time for fear is over, the time to listen to your intuition is now. The inner bridge that connects our souls is one you can create and dis-create. The crystal being today that represents that connectivity is kyanite. Strong and beautiful, it has many layers, as do you. The highest layer is love. Love comes from within, and is necessary to complete the bridge from your end. Many things will fall around today, but the love that connects us all will continue, for it is true is all dimensions. Do not be afraid. We are always here and we love you. The great light beings from beyond this dimension are watching over you giving you opportunities to explore this truth. Walk in faith, love and gratitude and watch your best life unfold.'-StarChild 3-2-12

"The crystal beings are here to communicate – you can learn a lot about the world you live in by being in communication with us. Today the crystal being Labradorite has come to remind you of the beauty and magic in your life – see the world with this magic and your life will transform' – StarChild 3-1-12

Where do we go from here?

The vortex of 11-11-11 has long passed, but the transition to the new realm has begun. The crystal skulls have held the promise of this era and are now here to show the way of love, light, harmony and peace. As we leave the 'dark' age behind us and enter this new era of light, the crystal skulls remind us that we are all connected through the light. May we all learn to live in harmony and be in the vibration of love that binds all of life throughout the dimensions.

Everyone has their own mission on this planet. Each person has a gift that is theirs to bless the world with. Some of you will become or have already become guardians of a crystal skull. May you always remember that it is a relationship, not merely an object, and the consciousness is always there, waiting to communicate and relate. The communication may come in the form of 'knowing,' or telepathic communication.

There is great power in the skulls, for they are not of this earth. They are here for only benevolent purposes, as using them for ego-based desires will only lead to issues of self healing as they are incapable of evil.

Many skulls both on and off planet participate in the monthly meditation for peace, held on the 13th of each month, at the 13th hour of the day (1PM local time). The crystal skull explorers facilitate this monthly event. Tap in to the energy of love and peace, you do not need to have a crystal skull to participate, but open yourself to peaceful, loving harmonics that invite the vibration of all to increase. The more people that participate in this construct of love and peace, the sooner it will come about. Energy radiates quanta into the field. The more quanta of a particular energy there is, the easier it becomes to resonate with that energy.

As we call in this new way of light, our descendants will know we took the steps to create this energetic quanta for them to create even higher forms of living on this planet-being, Earth. When there are no more wars or hunger, fear goes away and the healing of all forms of life reveals a new way to live. Oceans, skies and lands become clean again. And a new paradigm is born.

Know that any good energy that you put into the multiverse is always honored. You may never be aware of all the good that your loving prayers and meditation helped to happen. By removing yourself from the outcome, and focusing on the pure love and highest good of all, the process of manifesting reality occurs unobstructed by ego-based thoughts. We are learning to hone that process, and the crystal skulls are wonderful teachers.

Kindness is a natural by product of this type of energy. Be kind to the Earth, your fellow humans, the plants, animals, rock beings and all entities everywhere. It matters not what they have done to you, it is how you allow your energy to be affect by such actions. Transmute any negativity into forgiveness and love. Love each other, be kind, and direct your energetic flow in a positive way. Know that what ever is in your highest benefit will occur, even if it does not seem like it at the time. Trust and know that you are were you are meant to be.

You may consider becoming a guardian for a crystal skull. Your life could take off on an entirely new direction. Many people can trace the beginning of their awakening, or the beginning of huge growth, to their encounter with a crystal skull. There are resources in this publication should you wish to connect with one of those crystal beings.

Thank you for opening your heart in love and light. May you be blessed beyond what you can imagine.

StarChild's Facebook page:

https://www.facebook.com/MysticStarChildCrystalSkull?ref=hl

For more information about crystal skulls, or to purchase a high-quality crystal skull of your own, please see the Crystal Skull Explorers, Joshua Shapiro and Katrina Head and remember to participate in the monthly meditation for world peace.

Joshua and Katrina can be reached at:

http://www.whatarecrystalskulls.com

www.crystalskullexplorers.com
*
crystalskullexplorers@gmail.com.

free newsletter:
http://www.whoisjoshuashapiro.com/newsletter-signup.htm

free ebook:
http://www.v-j-enterprises.com/free-ebook/csexplorers.html

To reach Pamela Panneton of Landspirits for spiritual journeys, past life regression therapy, shamanic ceremony and healing

www.landspirits.com

Acknowledgements

There are so many I am grateful to in this labor of love. Thank you to Joshua Shapiro and Katrina Head, the Crystal Skull Explorers, for connecting me to my beloved StarChild, and being instrumental in the synchronicity of this even being possible. To their StarChildren, especially Rosalita, Portal, Geronimo and King/Lealani, for transmitting the information to StarChild and for transmitting their love to the world. To the Galactic Federation of Light, for making this part of my assignment on this beautiful blue globe, I thank you. To my guides, thank you, for this service has added great joy to my soul. To my friends and family who have been with me through this evolution of guardianship, thank you. Your love and support mean the world to me. And to you, dear reader, for reading this book. May you be lifted and supported as well as you find that which resonates with you. Thank you for making this world a more beautiful place to be.

About the Author:

Dr Linda Hostalek was born and raised near Chicago, but was open to exotic travel and mystical experiences from a young age. Mostly self-taught from a young age, her love of art and spirituality co-mingles in her art, books, and healing work. Most of her painting are made with holy water and contain the a vibrational essence of healing within them. She is a crystal skull guardian for StarChild, a trained cranial osteopath and holistic physician, as well as a master ceremonialist, trained in the Andes and jungles of Peru, Equator, Mexico and England, by some of the best healers in this world. She has taught shamanic apprenticeships and continues to find joy in traveling, painting, and in helping others achieve their healing.

She now makes her home on the Big Island of Hawaii, where she spends her days in spiritual communication with nature as she writes and paints, and does her healing work. For more information, to see her gallery of art or to read her holistic blog, please go to:

www.holisticwellnesshawaii.vpweb.com

'Be happy and be blessed, for joy is in your heart. It is up to you to acknowledge it.'

Linda Hostalek D.O.

Bonus Material

This contains extra material from StarKeepers. This happened over the summer of 2013, and is compatible to the StarChild channels that Linda receives near daily. This Gift to you is to help you to further explore the phenomenon of the star family and to help integrate them into your life.

These represent posts from the StarKeepersllc blog, and are added here as a gift to you. As a reminder, some of these may need to be read 'backwards' as they are from the blog. You can also go to the website to read them in their entirety, and to see any new updates as they are added.

Bless.

www.starkeepersllc.com

The Channels from StarKeepers
by Linda Hostalek D.O.

White ship seen over Hawaii

Today the white ship appeared. The Buddhist lantern ceremony of honoring ancestors and loved ones who have transitioned was performed today in a lovely Hawaii bay. The chantings and prayers from the Buddhist monk were powerful as the lanterns were lighted and all prayed together in unison. As the lanterns were lovingly placed in the water, the sight was magical as they began to float out into the bay, and out through the inlet and out to the open sea. I watched as angels guided the souls who were set free in the lighted lanterns, and set out to sea.

As the first round of lanterns came, a large white bird being flew by, taking the souls to the next realm. When the next wave of lanterns floated by, the bird being returned for their souls as well. The angels continued to free the lanterns that were caught on the rocks. It was then that the white ship appeared in the northwest sky. The wind began to blow and the lanterns were freed and set out to sea. As they passed the inlet, the white bird being again returned, signifying they were all taken to the next realm.

The white ship is the ship of the 'bird people,' so called because they are often observed as bird headed humans. They may also appear as winged angels, or as humanoid with large talons where a human's feet would be. They deliver a pure, high vibration of love and purity, and reminds us to be pure and holy as well. It is through their realm that we pass through to the next dimension. Many have encountered this star family without even knowing it. It is time to be more mindful of the encounters now.

The lanterns continued out to the open sea as the waves crashed against the shore as the stars shone above. The white ship stayed there for only a few moments, just to let us all know it was there. Most were too focused on the lanterns floating in the sea to take notice of the sky. It was approximately 7:25 pm Hawaii time.

Expect to see increased encounters with birds and flying creatures over the next several days. Emulate the behavior that resonates with you to fully take advantage of the energies present.

They said that many various Star Families will be returning to connect with those here on Earth. Those with family roots in Sirius and Orion will notice the next wave more pronounced than others, although all will feel the presence if mindful. This is in part due to the need for their help in overcoming the tragic ways humans are treating each other. It is time to restore the harmony, love and kindness so that there may peace, and our planet being restored back to health.

It is time to realize that we are much more

similar than we are different, in fact we are one family, as we all come from the stars. It is time to release the pettiness and get on with the business of restoring peace. Take time to connect to one's star family through communication with nature, by looking to the sky, and by listening to the small, still voice within. It is given to us for a reason.

The white ship did not indicate when it would return, but did indicate more waves of sightings will begin soon, and to keep our eyes to the skies and our ears to the ground. There will soon be signs on the Earth that will speak to you. This may be the lighted path in a forest, or the rumblings of a quake, but the signs will begin within one week. Do not fear, this is only to remind you that you are so much more than the earthly body in which you inhabit currently.

Your DNA has been upgraded and is beginning to function. Abilities are strengthening within you as you connect with the natural world. This will continue and is part of the new normal of this era. You will begin to hear of humans who have what seems to be extraordinary abilities. Remember, that you, too, have abilities that are evolving, and as you listen to your star family's messages for you, you will develop those abilities more quickly.

Some may find that have either extra energy, or may be very tired, almost to the point of feeling drugged. This is due to the upgrades you are receiving, and will pass within the week. Try out what seems different to you, you may find your senses are improving, and that perhaps you can see better or hear better, or may heal faster or begin to receive messages.

The time table is an accelerated one. It is already here and now all are catching up with the soon to be future. Enjoy this time, it is preparing you for optimization of your gifts so that you may better serve. bless

I thought I would also include today's

StarChild channeling, as when I read it after today's events, it touched my heart. May your days be blessed. Starkeepers

Posted on August 26, 2013. | Tagged bird beings, bird people, galactic federation of light, orion, Sirian, star family, star keepers, white ship | Leave a comment | Edit

Golden Lyrian Ship sighted at Full Moon

It has been an incredible time of late. With the recent sighting of the red triangular ship, Star Family had made it clear that ships would also be present through the full moon. Many have reported seeing ships of differing sizes, shapes and colors throughout this time period. Last night, as we peered at the full moon, we saw a glittery golden ship. Sort of a truncated pyramidal shape, it was clear that it was from Lyra. This rarely seen ship has traveled far to bring us this message of Illumination. Contact was made again at 2:22 am, and was told that another contact, and the message would be delivered at 1:11pm, local time. In between the night and day times, we received confirmation that others have also seen this Golden ship, not only in Hawaii, but also on the east coast of the mainland, where many gathered and were witness to it.

At 1:10pm, I felt the ships presence and went to a tree overlooking the water, at 1:11pm, the transmission began:

The Tree had may branches reaching over the water, a sturdy trunk, and multiple, thick roots stretching over the land. I perched on one of the enormous roots and connected at that moment.

There are many expression of the Divine, one trunk and many roots. All is one, and although it may seem separate, in reality it is one essence.

The Golden light is the complement to the blue light that comes from and through the Pleiades. The Golden ray of Illumination, along with the Blue ray of healing and life, (including the ability to transfer between lives), combine in the green ray of love, harmony and peace, which vibrates through the plant beings to immerse this planet in love. There are 12 main vibrational essences, each along with a color, represented by various Star Families. These are analogous to the 12 strands of DNA which are vibrating with new light codes that were downloaded during the ascension phase over the past two years or so (the 'junk' DNA activation phase). Each strand contains a different element of color, and thus a different gift. This Golden Ray is representative of the Lyrian Star Family, but has been represented in the past as ArchAngel Michael, the golden warrior angel, whose armor glows as gold as his sword cuts to the truth, and slays the lies.

The Lyrians are the cat beings. That

primal Divine Feline Energy has been represented as that of Bat, the Egyptian Cat Goddess, or as Sacred Tigers in the Himalayas, or Jaguars in the Americas. The essence of this feline energy is one that is powerful enough to slay, but gentle enough to cuddle and purr. It is this essence that has come in power, strength and beauty. This is to make all aware that we carry both sides of the energies, and it is our choice as to which aspect of the energy comes through.

Choose the love, as this what this transformative period is all about. Transformation through Illumination. This is the Golden Ray of Illumination delivered by the Golden Lyrian Ship. Those who have seen this ship will see it again, and it precedes the arrival of the white ship of the bird people. (There was no mention when this would occur)

To vibrate with this Lyrian Cat-like energy, we are reminded to stretch our bodies, lay in the sun, be finicky with what we ingest, move in a way that the energy feels better, and to be comfortable in your own 'skin.' Retain the flexibility of a cat in all aspects of the body, mind and spirit. Notice if you can see better in the dark, or if you can balance better. Can you hear the spirit's voice and intuit the essences of creatures of the night. The void is ripe with infinite possibilities. What you create is up to you. Embrace this energy as in becomes ones with your essence. You will then be ready to meet the white ship when it arrives. bless

JAGUAR PYRAMID
LINDA HOSTALEK D.O.

Posted on August 22, 2013. | Tagged Cat, contact, energy, ETs. contact, Feline, full moon, galactic federation of light, Jaguar, Lyrian, Pleiades, Sirian, star family, Tiger | Leave a comment | Edit

Star Family Update

It has been an exciting week! Triangular ships seen in Joshua Tree, other people have also reported seeing red ships, white ships and golden ones. The message is one of harmony, peace and love. Vibrate high as we create this new age of light. Contact will continue through the full moon, so keep your eyes to the skies and let us know what you see! bless

Posted on August 14, 2013. | Tagged contact, ETs, full moon, galactic federation, harmony, light, love, peace, ships, star family, UFOs | Leave a comment | Edit

Confirmation of ships sighted at Joshua Tree

We have just received news from Blake and Brent Cousins of Third Phase Moon (those who did our video, see previous post) of confirmation that an arrow shaped ship was seen at Joshua Tree this weekend. This was observed at the UFO conference by Steven Greer, as reported to us from the Cousin brothers. Just thought you would want to know. Please let us know if you know of other sightings during this time. Thank you. bless

Posted on August 12, 2013. | Tagged confirmation, ETs, hawaii, Pleaides, sirius, star family, stars, UFO contact | Leave a comment | Edit

UFO Sightings Leaked Info Massive UFO Event? Special Report 2013

The red triangular ships have made themselves known. In conjunction with other events throughout the globe, lets all vibrate together in love, peace and harmony. bless

Posted on August 11, 2013. | Tagged contact, hawaii, Sirians, Star FAmily Update, triangular ships, UFOs | Leave a comment | Edit

Star Family Update

Star Family Update

Message came through yesterday regarding a triangular red ship that will be present for the next several days. We were told to look in the northeast – that it will be anywhere from the east to the north. At 4:44 am the ship appeared, and yellow and red light were seen which came in from the east. The message was that more contact will be made over the next seven days. There are messages being delivered to people who have been open and ready to receive contact from their star family. The numbers are harboring the sacred codes of contact, and people are encouraged to notice the numbers, especially the time, related to 4. Therefore, multiples of 4, including 8, 16, 32, 64, etc, are to be paid attention to. There is an impending push through of that which has been worked towards. For example, projects which are from the stars that those connected have been directed are about to come to fruition. Expect barriers to be removed in the most unusual way, and for the star family to continue the guidance to see these project through. People of Earth – prepare to be participants in the restoration of this being Earth. Through listening to the sacredness of the water, plants and animals as well as the signs in the sky and earth, the holiness is restored and brought once again back in to balance. You are key to this change. You are becoming more and more open and your vibration has been calibrated to this change. That is why things are manifesting in a more timely manner for humans at this time. The DNA is activated and is now integrating the new human in to the programming. It is a most exciting time as the barriers are removed and the guidance is here. Look to the sky, especially the north east (but anywhere from the north to the east) for the lights in the sky to confirm this for you. They will be visible for the next seven days. Much is going on on this globe and people are seeking the answers – which are being delivered to you at this time now. So, be actively listening, your star family is calling. Those with connections from Sirius will feel this the most. Be aware and journey forth. The numbers open dimensional pathways by creating a portal for contact. Notice what stands out for you. bless.

Posted on **August 10, 2013**. | Tagged numerology, portals, sacred, ships, sirius, star family, UFOs | 2 Comments | Edit

Sacredness in all around you

It has been an interesting time, many people are experiencing contact in varying forms, many involving requests from the natural world for help in loving them back to health, specifically the pollinators and the sea creatures have been making contact. Remember there are undersea bases that communicate with the ships and the whale beings and the dolphin beings, at times, are intermediaries between the worlds. July 27th is the day to hold the ocean family, and the undersea bases in your thoughts and prayers. Together as we raise the collective vibration in light and love, may their restoration occur. Please consider joining us on line at

In addition, this came transmission came in regarding a very special place here on the Big Island of Hawaii, one valley over from the sacred valley Waipio, called Wanamanu (spelling?) I am still in awe of this transmission, and when we receive further instructions regarding this we will proceed (as in the event above for the ocean family). Much love to you all, and mahalo, thank you, for your continued love and support.

July 13, 2013

Waimanu valley
valley of the stars/the ancient ones calling

There is a very holy place in Waimanu valley asking for a code for the star gate to activate. The code came to me and it was spoken by us. The dimensional doorways shifted, and as it did, we could see the ancient starship, disc shaped, silver, with the symbols which by now are familiar to us, beaming energy to the sacred ground which was at one time an ancient altar, about 2/3 of the way up from the valley floor and somewhat inland on the right if looking from the ocean. This altar is to this day attended to by stone beings, who look somewhat similar to rocks and tikis. This ship beamed golden light to this altar, which then changed to the blue light that carries the consciousness of love and the life force. This altar area also contained many plants, some of which were retrieved by the ship and taken aboard. These particular plants are filled with a great deal of mana, or life force energy, kauwsi, prana, etc, and this energy was permeated throughout this sacred valley as well. Some of the plants in this altar area have a blue tinge, but most were green, and carry the green ray of love which permeates the plant kingdom with love and healing. Similar episodes have happened to the other sacred axis mundi of the world and the sacred plants all carry this golden into blue light of holy consciousness. This is why the ceremonies and traditions carry similar vibrations of holiness throughout this world and the others as well. All are connected. This sacred mana feed the spirit of the beings throughout this planet. The blue light went down far underground and re emerged in the plant kingdom, through the roots, in the seaweed, kelp, trees, bushes, ferns, etc. to carry the life-force of love. Tend to the plants and listen to them for they are the keepers of the energy of the ancient wisdom and ways now being rediscovered. The codes are in them, and particular plants have been seeded with perfect knowledge of love. Some of these holy plants are awa, ayahuasca in the jungle, native tobacco, ferns, taro, kokua nut tree, blue jade vine, maile vine, bromeliads, ferns, orchids, some cacti (although not in this particular valley), to name but a few. This vibration of the blue light is part of the reason why the oceans appear blue, and why the green ray of love (the mixture of teh golden ray and the blue) is within the plants. It is also why they must be conserved and treated with the love and respect they deserve. The ancient wisdom has been contained in the plants, and was seeded here over 26,000 years ago. It is now the entry into the light cycle of the new golden age that this star-gate has now been made known and this knowledge is available to all and for all. This is also why the supplications and prayers for healing all aspects of this planet is so imperative. The healing is held in the plants, the waters in them and their flowers and essences as well. Prayers for a balanced and healthy ecosystem are made. Gratitude to the stone beings from the previous dimensions who have held the space and guarded this sacred altar's entrance of this powerful and beautiful star-gate. It is now open and blesses the world with it's love. The blue light is the light that animates all life and how beings travel through dimensions and in between the 'lives' they live. This will be made more freely available as this cycle of the light continues. Love your plants, they feed your soul and spirit. A healthy forest is a healthy planet, heal the waters. I see dolphins, whales, canoe, waterfalls on either side of the altar tended to by stone beings. Inter-dimensional healing is occurring now on this planet, and will continue. the divine hears our prayers, and our star-family has come to greet us and make themselves known. Thank you for this holy vision of light and love. Mahalo Ke Akua. Bless.

Reynolds and I then did a ceremony and the swirling light engulfed us. The plants merged with us, and in Reynolds heart area, appeared a heart shaped leaf, which looked like a taro leaf. I was struck by how much vessels, like blood vessels and nerve 'trees' look like plants. Very, very special. Thank you, as I am still shaking from this most lovely of experiences. bless.

I HOLD YOU IN MY HANDS
LINSA HOSTALEK D.O.

StarChild Photo Gallery

StarChild in Santa Fe, NM 2012

StarChild with Geronimo, San Juan Islands, WA May 2012

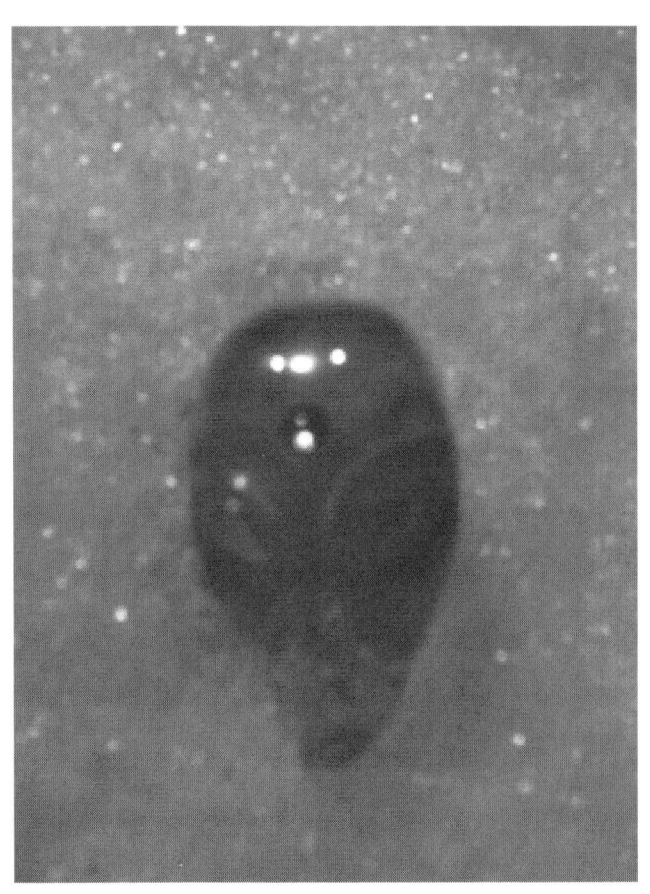

StarChild in snow on the holy mountain
Mount Rainer, outside Seattle, May 2012

StarChild, baptized in the Cathedral, Santa Fe, NM March 2012

StarChild in Hawaii with her guardian,
Linda Hostalek 2013

'Be happy and be blessed, for joy is in your heart. It is up to you to acknowledge it.'

Linda Hostalek D.O.

Printed in Great Britain
by Amazon.co.uk, Ltd.,
Marston Gate.